*There's a*
# PORCUPINE
*in My*
# OUTHOUSE

*There's a*
# PORCUPINE
*in My*
# OUTHOUSE

*The Vermont Misadventures*
*of a Mountain Man Wannabe*

MICHAEL J. TOUGIAS

LYONS
PRESS

Guilford, Connecticut

An imprint of Globe Pequot, the trade division of
The Rowman & Littlefield Publishing Group, Inc.
4501 Forbes Blvd., Ste. 200
Lanham, MD 20706
www.rowman.com

Distributed by NATIONAL BOOK NETWORK

British Library Cataloguing in Publication Information available

Library of Congress Cataloging-in-Publication Data available

ISBN 978-1-4930-6365-9 (paper : alk. paper)
ISBN 978-1-4930-6366-6 (electronic)

# CONTENTS

To Cogs and Boomer

# PREFACE

In 1978, when I was twenty-two, I spent $8,500 on a tiny A-frame cabin and six acres of land overlooking a pond in northern Vermont. I thought I would live out my mountain-man fantasy that had been planted in my mind from reading adventure books as a kid. I would be Jim Bridger, Daniel Boone, and Lewis and Clark all rolled into one, knowing exactly what to do in every outdoor situation. I fancied myself as lord and master of my six acres. My very first act as a landowner was to go out and chop down a tree.

Now, many years later, I look back at those early years at the cabin and realize I had it backward. I haven't controlled the land or conquered it, but instead I've been humbled by what I learned about nature, even though I've barely begun to understand its rhythms and many mysteries. This ramshackle cabin has been a kind of university for my outdoor education, although I am far from graduating. I think I will be a lifelong student, grateful for each and every unexpected lesson. I've experienced encounters with wildlife from bears to bats, friendships with life-hardened locals and neophyte flatlanders, terror at being lost in the woods, moments that require true ingenuity, and a greater awareness of that incredible commodity-time. Time to explore the natural world and time to reflect inward, questioning paths chosen.

It didn't occur to me to write a book about the cabin and my observations until I started to get letters from readers of my weekly outdoor column. Normally, I'd rarely hear from readers, but whenever I wrote about the cabin I would invariably receive several letters. They would encourage me to write more about my "shack on the mountain" and the adventures and misadventures that occurred there. Some readers even wrote asking if they could rent the cabin, saying they wanted a vacation that involved roughing it, that they liked the idea of an outhouse! After I received dozens of these notes, I took a look at my cabin's guest book and journal and decided to tell the story of my first few years at the cabin. This book is a chronicle of growth during my twenties, mistakes I made along the way, and my evolution from the concept of "conquering" the land to one of stewardship. I wrote it with a light touch because some of the things I did are a bit embarrassing, and now that I'm in my sixties I've learned to go easy on myself. Hopefully, you will too.

# CHAPTER 1

# THE FIRST TRIP

*I don't know what we bought or where it is.*

My lifelong dream had come true: I had bought a cabin in the mountains. The only problem was that I couldn't find it.

The first time I saw the unheated A-frame was in December when I purchased it, and now it was April, time for my first overnight stay. I recruited my brother Bob to accompany me, and we left our Massachusetts home in the wee hours of the morning, bursting with excitement to be mountain men for a weekend. I was twenty-two and Bob was sixteen. With years of backyard camping under our belts, we both considered ourselves outdoorsmen.

Our first shock on that spring morning was that while the lawns in suburban Massachusetts were turning green with new growth, the hills of Vermont were cloaked in snow. To make matters worse, the roads oozed thick mud, the consistency of chocolate pudding. Being a flatlander, I had never experienced mud season, but as we left the paved roads of Montpelier and headed into the woods on dirt lanes, the meaning was explicit. The lanes were a soupy mess; moisture in the upper layers of the soil had nowhere to drain, because the ground below was still frozen. We were in my father's 1971 Ford station wagon, a big boat of a car with fake-wood-paneled sides, that had a tendency to fishtail in the muck. The mud got deeper with every passing mile until we dared not go any farther.

Parking on what appeared to be a firm shoulder, we hoisted backpacks filled with overnight gear to walk the last few miles. On one side of the lane was an alder swamp, where beavers had made a series of dams, while the other side was a steep wooded ridge that blocked out the late afternoon sun. The thrill of showing Bob my new purchase gave me extra energy, and we covered the first two miles quickly. In my hand was a crude map with landmarks I had sketched last December after snowshoeing in with the realtor who guided me to the cabin. I explained to Bob for the hundredth time that the cabin was nothing fancy. "It's the location that counts," I said again. My A-frame sat high on a ridge overlooking a twenty-five-acre spring-fed pond.

As we rounded the corner the pond came into view, and I felt like a proud new father, pointing at the far hillside that encompassed the six acres I'd bought. I hadn't expected the pond to be ice-covered still, but no matter, we were finally there. Or were we? At the far side of the pond, where there should have been a narrow road winding up to the cabin, there was nothing but a thick stand of hemlock and spruce trees.

"Isn't the driveway supposed to be here?" asked Bob, looking over my shoulder at the map.

I almost choked him. Of course it was. I examined my little map. Everything else was in place; the road ran alongside the pond and the stream exited the back of the pond—our private lane should have crossed over the stream and headed up the hill.

"Maybe it's down the road a little farther," I murmured.

We kept walking the roadway, searching to our right for the little lane that would cross the stream. I noticed there were only a couple of tire marks in the mud and that we hadn't passed a home or cabin since we abandoned the car. After stopping a couple more times to look at the map, I said, "Maybe we missed it, let's go back."

I knew we hadn't, but I didn't know what else to do. Back at the pond, I scanned the unwelcoming rugged brown hills with their patches of rotten snow. No sign of my cabin anywhere. I started to look at the pond more closely. It looked smaller than

I remembered, and it was shallow, with alders poking up through the ice even near its center. A beaver dam walled off the pond from the stream, and it appeared that if the dam crumbled, the pond would go with it. My heart sank; not only was there no cabin, but the pond—*our pond*—was more a swamp than the "liquid jewel" I'd been describing to anyone who would listen.

Bob took off his backpack. "We could try to cross the stream and bushwhack up the hill."

I shook my head; the stream was roaring with runoff—there was no way to cross it. "I swear there was some kind of road, or at least a trail, that crossed the stream over a culvert and went up the hill. The realtor even said you could drive up in the summer."

There was an awkward silence. Bob had a blank look on his face, kicking at a pile of the snow the plow had left. I was wondering how we would explain to our father that we couldn't find our property. "Well, Dad," I would say, "we had a little problem—the cabin is missing." No, that sounded ridiculous; maybe, "the private road to the cabin is gone, so we had to come home." Not much better, but still preferable to the truth: "I don't know what we bought or where it is."

I was definitely feeling more like a city slicker than the mountain man I'd ventured out to be.

Bob tried a new approach. "When you were here in December, how did you get up the driveway with all this snow?"

"The realtor had snowshoes in her trunk."

"So you didn't actually see the driveway, because it was covered with snow."

"What are you getting at?" I snapped.

"Maybe there is no driveway. Maybe there was so much snow it just looked like a driveway, and you just snowshoed over the stream on a log."

"It wasn't a log, it was . . ."

A thought occurred to me. I stuck my nose back in the map. What if Bob and I hadn't trudged far enough? Maybe this wasn't our pond.

"Listen," I stammered, "I might be wrong about this pond. Maybe it's not the right one. Let's keep walking."

I didn't wait for him to answer, but trudged on up the muddy road, the sucking sound of my boots mocking me. Our little walk now felt like a major expedition.

Where the road crested a hill we paused to fish our water bottles out of our packs and drank greedily. I was secretly hoping a car would pass so we could ask for a ride or directions, but there was no sign of life anywhere, not even a bird in a tree, let alone other humans. Dark hemlocks and spruce crowded the road, casting shadows even though it was mid-afternoon, and the sun had pushed the temperature into the low fifties. I was drenched in sweat and told Bob we'd give it ten more minutes.

As the road curved to the right around a slate ledge, I saw the most welcome sight of my young life.

"That's it, that's it!" I shouted, "That's my pond!" We moved quickly now, down the road then over the stream on our narrow private lane and up the hill. As we crested the ridge, we saw the lonely looking A-frame cabin perched on the wooded hilltop. We had made it!

When we got closer I saw that towering hemlock, spruce, and fir trees blocked most of the view of the pond below. What little paint the cabin had was peeling, and I could see a big crack in the kitchen window. I use the term "kitchen" rather loosely; while my little cabin had a sink, there was no well, no water, and no plumbing.

Bob and I laid our packs on the four-foot-wide-by-eight-foot-long porch and went inside, turning on the lights. There was no water, but we did have electricity. (In years to come, many a guest would be temporarily fooled by the sink and ask where the shower and bathroom were.) Bob slowly walked around the single large room, touching the exposed beams on the wall, pushing away cobwebs from the back window, which would not open for him. It appeared as if the previous owners had not used the place for at least a year. If Bob was disappointed he didn't show it, but simply said, "We can fix this up; it's got potential." And it did have a lot of potential, but not much else. The walls were unfinished plywood, and the only insulation was hanging from the ceiling. In addition to the cracked window in the front, there were two windows in the back, and the entire first floor was one big room. It was empty except for four old, but comfortable, oak chairs. A set of pull-down stairs from the ceiling allowed access to the second floor, which was also one big unfinished room with a couple of windows.

So what did I do first? With such a Spartan situation, you would think I'd have taken measurements for insulating the walls, or hanging ceiling panels, or installing a future woodstove. Instead, I cut down a tree.

Bob sat on the porch, drinking a can of Coke, watching me take my hatchet out of my pack, walk over to a small yellow birch, and start hacking. He raised his eyebrows, the look on his face implying that I'd lost my mind, but there was a method to my madness. For me, a mountain man was a rugged individual carving out his place in the forest. The tree I chose was close to the cabin, but not blocking the view and not in any danger of falling into the cabin; still, I needed to take down a tree and this was the closest.

I had a lot to learn about my relationship with the outdoors and even more to learn about cutting down a tree. Although the birch was no wider than my thigh, it took me a solid hour of chopping with my dull hatchet to get more than halfway. I kept chopping, and when I noticed it tilting a bit, I gave it a shove. The birch moaned, then cracked, and I leapt away as it came crashing down. By that time dusk had settled in and the air was cool, and I had forgotten why I needed to cut it down in the first place.

Bob had gathered dead branches from a spruce, made a fire in the tiny clearing in front of the cabin, and had our hot dogs roasting when I keeled over from exhaustion. We dragged the oak chairs outside and gobbled down three hot dogs each, realizing that an outdoor setting and lots of hiking can make even a hot dog taste wonderful. Staring into the flames, I looked forward to days to come, knowing I was well on my way to being a mountain man. I had blisters on my hands and a dead tree to prove it.

A little one-seater outhouse sat about fifty feet behind the cabin. It was in rough shape, tilting ever so slightly to the right side; the door didn't close properly and the roof sagged a bit. On my first visit to the little structure, I found that the seat was too far off the floor for me to sit comfortably and my feet dangled two inches above the plywood floor. But at least there was no offensive smell. In fact, it had a pleasant evergreen scent, and I noticed pellets spilling out an opening in the back. What a great idea, I thought. The former owners had filled the "hole" with pine-scented pellets. *I'll have to add these to my shopping list.*

I sat down to answer nature's call, and smiled when I saw that one whole side of the outhouse was filled with firewood, all split and dried. I knew it would have taken me three years to amass that much wood with my hatchet. A noise startled me as I considered the cost of chainsaws. The sound was directly below me. I jumped about a mile in the air, stumbling to the floor with pants wrapped around my ankles. The noise stopped. I felt rather embarrassed by my reaction—it was only a soft rustling noise, probably a mouse scurrying in the leaves below.

Back at the fire, Bob commented how lucky we were to have down-filled sleeping bags, as the temperature had dropped into the thirties. We decided to sleep on the porch, because the inside of the cabin was dank and musty, feeling colder than outside after being closed up all winter. It was only 8:00 P.M., but there wasn't a heck of a lot to do after the conversation died out, so we called it a night. We donned hats and crawled into our bags fully clothed, falling asleep almost immediately.

Sometime in the middle of the night a piercing scream split the icy air, and every hair on my skinny little body stood straight up. It sounded like someone was being murdered ten feet from the porch. My heart was pounding, but I couldn't move a muscle. The hatchet was still in the stump of the tree I'd cut (or in the person who had just been murdered), and I had no way of protecting us from becoming the next victims. Why did I want be a mountain man? In my frightened state I just wanted to be safe in my bed at home in the suburbs, not out here in the middle of nowhere.

Bob whispered first. "What was that?"

I'd forgotten about Bob. Thank God for good old Bob. There were two of us to fight or two of us to run, and I was faster.

"Ssssshhhhhh," I answered. I didn't want to be heard.

I eased my arm out of the sleeping bag, groping for the flashlight. When I had it in my hand, I allowed myself to exhale.

"Aaaaayyyyyyyyyyyyy!!!!!!!" Another scream let loose. This one was closer to us. With flashlight beam waving wildly, I rolled to my left, pitched off the porch, hit the ground with a thud, and scrambled out of my sleeping bag. I didn't run. I couldn't. My legs were shaking too hard and I felt faint. Instead I stood and scanned the woods with my flashlight, but could see nothing.

Another scream—this time right over my head! I dropped to the ground and aimed the light in the tree. *Oh God,* I whimpered, *what is this thing?* Then one—no two—pairs of red eyes shined back at me.

The shape of the creatures came into focus. Porcupines. They were side by side, looking down at me. I'd interrupted something—maybe they were mating and a quill had touched a sensitive area. By now I was drenched in nervous sweat, and I laughed at myself in relief.

Bob crawled out of the bottom of his sleeping bag and stood beside me. "Will you look at that?" he whispered, "I didn't know porcupines could talk."

Before he said anything more, the porcupines were on the move, awkwardly coming down the tree. We stood back, keeping the light trained on them, and then safely followed behind as they lumbered into the back of the outhouse, through the opening where the pine-scented pellets spilled out.

Then it hit me. The shuffling noise I'd heard during my earlier visit to the outhouse was the sound of porcupines living under it. My mind played through the possible scenarios involving my exposed body parts and porcupine quills—I was luckier than I realized.

We all know that porcupines cannot throw their quills. But wait a minute—they can swing their tails, and the one in the hole could have swiped his tail across my butt. That's twenty-five thousand quills. If there were two porcupines, it's fifty thousand. True, not all fifty thousand are going to be delivered into my butt. But all it takes is one to do me great harm. And here's the other crucial point—if a porcupine can nip a branch off in one bite . . .

Now you're probably saying, *Boy, does this guy have an imagination.* But I'll bet somewhere, sometime, someone's run into an emergency room with porcupine quills attached to their butt. It's just not the kind of story that makes the papers or the evening news. And it's not the kind of story you brag about. But you can be sure the nurses and doctors in the E.R. had a good laugh, probably thinking the accident was the result of some kinky sexual experimentation. Go ahead and laugh, but my wife is a nurse and she says stranger cases have happened.

A porcupine quill has a razor-sharp point and a hollow, air-filled pocket. The shaft of the quill is covered with microscopic barbs that can work deeper and deeper into the flesh, eventually traveling through the victim's body. People who try to pet a cute-looking porcupine often remark, "I was surprised how fast it swung its tail." People who use a porcupine den as an outhouse usually say, "I had no idea it could reach my butt."

Even if the porcupine in my outhouse couldn't reach me with his tail, it could still get me with one of those hollow spears. I'd read that with a flip of its tail a porcupine could send an old quill flying as much as five or six feet, like a flying dart. I also learned that these fifteen- to thirty-pound rodents not only can scream, but also can moan, whine, grunt, and cough. Like most animals, porcupines have their social periods, and when females are checking out prospective mates, size matters. Mating is a selective practice, and the female is very choosy. Rick Sweitzer, a biologist at the University of California, Davis, reports in *National Wildlife* that "one way she [the female porcupine] might select her mate is by visually assessing male vigor or quality based on quill size or density."

Obviously, the female controls which male has all the fun. With twenty-five thousand quills, she can deny her suitor any contact of the intimate kind. But when the female finds a mate to her liking, they dance awhile. (Both stand on their hind legs, touch noses, and rock back and forth.) Then, if the dancing is acceptable, she will back up to the male and raise her tail. About two hundred days later a porcupette is born (that's really what baby porcupines are called), and together they will den in rocky crevices (or under outhouses), spending most of their day sleeping before emerging at night to feed.

I was to learn a lot about porcupines—and life—over the next few years. Bob and I managed to go back to sleep that night and left the next morning, but before doing so we started an important tradition—writing down our experiences in the guest book. Later entries average about a page, but the first one was rather short and cryptic.

### *April 20*
*Had to park three miles away 'cause of the mud. Couldn't find cabin at first. Freezing cold last night. Next guest should not use the outhouse until further notice.*

# CHAPTER 2

# MOUNTAIN MADNESS:
# LOVE OF THE LAND,
# FEAR OF THE NIGHT

*I am here alone and enjoying it, although last night when I
had to return to the car I carried two flashlights, a hatchet,
a shovel, and the bass spear. I love a night in the forest. . . .*
—ENTRY IN GUEST BOOK

On my first trip alone to the cabin I discovered my desire to learn
all I could about nature—including the discovery that I was afraid
of bears. I returned in May, about a month after Bob and I visited, and it seemed as though the forest had awakened and exploded with life. As I sauntered over the land, everything seemed new
and fresh, and the earth became a place of enchantment, full of
possibilities and endless adventures.

Fiddlehead ferns poked up from the leaf mold, and the newly
unfurled leaves of the birches, maples, and beeches cast a light
green hue, so distinctive in May. Birdcalls rang out and a pileated
woodpecker swooped from its drumming on a dead tree, bright-
ening the woods with its red crest. I was now a landowner and
this was my land—the sense of satisfaction and contentment was
indescribable. It was a heady experience, and I felt that here was
the special place I had been looking for.

Traversing the steep ridge that runs from the front of the cabin toward the east and drops over two hundred feet down to the pond, I felt like a newly crowned king greeting his subjects. I stopped and admired the smooth gray bark of the beeches, rubbing my hand on their cool trunks like a rider stroking his horse. Under a particularly large hemlock, I sat on the ground and looked up at the majestic sweep of its branches. At the highest point on the ridge a lone white pine, a true giant, stood like a sentinel. I wondered how it had escaped the farmer's axe a century ago. I knew that like almost every acre in New England, my land had likely been pasture in the nineteenth century and that true old-growth forest tracts were now few and far between.

As I walked I noted how different trees dominated different acres, and saw where trillium graced the forest floor. For the first time I paused long enough to see how firs could be distinguished from spruce by their tightly pointed crowns, and how little undergrowth grew beneath the hemlocks. I observed the rounded crown of the sugar maples and the bright white bark of the paper birches. This walk was the start of my nature education, learning through patient observation. I made a pact with myself to carry a guidebook to tree identification from now on so that I could find the answers to questions that eluded me, such as the reason why undergrowth struggles beneath hemlocks (the tree's fallen needles are acidic).

I was to learn that I was not the king of those six acres, but merely the temporary caretaker. The land, I came to see, owned me, and I was just the loyal subject whose mission it was to protect it. But all that came years later when the concept of ownership was replaced by the knowledge that I was simply passing through. It was the land that was permanent, not me.

I tramped far and wide that day, going way off my property and into the hills on the west side of the pond before turning back as the sun set. In my daypack was a field guide to animal tracks, and in the mud by the pond I identified the tracks of mink, beavers, and raccoons. I was thrilled to find such diverse signs of wildlife, until I circled around and came up the "driveway"—the five-hundred-yard road up the hill to the cabin that Bob and I had had such a difficult time finding. (The road was only suitable for four-wheel-drive vehicles, so I'd left my car down by the pond.) On the driveway I saw enormous tracks going up the hill in the same direction as I was heading. *Must be a large dog,* I told myself. But when I flipped through the guidebook to the "B" section, there was little doubt as to what had lumbered ahead of me. Beavers, mink, raccoons, and even the porcupine I had expected here, but not something bigger, stronger, and with more teeth than me. I hadn't counted on a bear.

The realtor had never said a thing about this. What happened to full disclosure? If a property has carpenter ants, realtors are required to tell you. Carpenter ants are bad, very bad, but they eat the house, not you. No, I did not count on a bear living here, especially not on my first night alone at the cabin.

Well, at least the bear (or *bears*—my tracking skills could not distinguish) would be outside and I would be inside. Then I thought of the porcupine. *If there's a porcupine living in my outhouse, it doesn't take a big leap of imagination to think a bear could be in the cabin.* My imagination was fueled by darkness, and at that moment, or so it seemed, someone had pulled a curtain down on the woods that had appeared so charming just hours earlier.

Have you ever noticed how quickly night closes in when you're in the woods? There's nothing gradual about it. One minute the birds are singing and the sun is above the mountaintops, and the next minute it drops like a rock. The foliage that brightens the forest with greenery now blocks out what little light is still left. The breeze ends as though someone turned off a large fan, and the woods become very still, and a little eerie.

I raced up the hill, hopped onto the cabin's porch, and tore open the backpack I had left there. Cookies, underwear, shaving cream, beer, a hat, pillow, and every manner of supplies fell out—except the one I was looking for. There was no flashlight. This was serious. It had been only three weeks earlier that I'd slept in this very same spot and heard the porcupine I almost sat on. I was imagining what would have happened that night if I had not had the flashlight and the courage it gave me to finally find out what made those hideous noises. Let me tell you. I'd be in Bellevue, drooling in a padded room where they don't allow sharp objects. And now here I was in a similar situation, with no flashlight and no Bob to outrun. And we're not talking pudgy little porcupine this time. I'm talking about a nocturnal prowling beast that can weigh up to six hundred pounds, who is probably resting nearby waiting for the right opportunity to pounce on the idiot who considered himself "king" of these six acres. I could picture the bear thinking to himself, *Who is this person that dares enter my territory, cutting down my favorite yellow birch?*

I went into the cabin and turned on the lights. There was no bear, of course. But here's the crucial point: The cabin rests on cinder blocks at each corner, which means three feet of open space lie beneath the structure, forming a dry, sheltered place—very cavelike. Bears live in caves, which means there could be one directly underneath the cabin, directly underneath where I was standing, clutching the stupid hatchet I'd brought. The very same hatchet that cut down the bear's favorite yellow birch. The tree he probably rubbed his fur against, the tree he probably rested under on hot days, the tree he might have regarded as a friend. And now the bear thinks, *This human is here, and he cut the tree, and he's a flatlander geek from Massachusetts, and . . .* OK, maybe I was getting a little carried away. But understand what was going through my mind that night. I was there by myself and wondering why. Indeed, at that moment, had someone knocked on the door I would have had a heart attack. And if that particular someone had said, "Hey, you've got a nice cabin," I would have answered, "Here's the key; it's yours if you'll stay here tonight with me."

Oh sure, I can hear you saying it again: *What an imagination this guy's got. He actually thinks there's a bear under his cabin. Next thing he'll say is there's a bobcat in his cupboard.*

Go ahead, make fun of me. But remember this: Whose outhouse had a porcupine living in it? Is it so hard to understand why I might think a bear could be under the cabin?

I picked up my guidebook hoping to locate some helpful

information. The first thing I read was how much bears like beechnuts. That didn't help—there are plenty of beech trees on my land. Even more disturbing was the guidebook's description of the bear's climbing ability, stating that they can and do climb trees. That's one more escape route closed. With my luck, I would climb a tree upon hearing a twig snap from a passing deer, only to meet a bear in the upper branches.

I barricaded the cabin door shut and thought how little the camping in my backyard had prepared me for these mountains. On half of those backyard outings I had wandered back into the house, and on all of them I had camped with a friend. Never alone, and certainly never in a cabin that had a bear sleeping under it.

Fortunately the day's hike succeeded in knocking me out and I slept like a log, until a mouse ran over my face. I screamed, thinking the bear had unlocked the door. I groped for my hatchet and could not find it, so I did the trusty commando roll in my sleeping bag, rolling right over my glasses and crushing them. Now I was as blind as a bat and only knew that *something*, probably the bear, was in the cabin with me. This was very serious. My quandary—whether to run outside or stay inside—was a lose-lose proposition. What was worse—staying in the cabin, knowing I was sharing it with another living creature, or going into the pitch-black woods with no flashlight? It was like the choices we used to quiz each other with as kids: Would you rather be eaten by a shark, or be covered in honey and tied to a mound of fire ants?

I decided to be a man and turn on the lights. There was no bear, but I did hear (I couldn't see without my glasses) the scurrying of what I was sure was a mouse. I breathed a sigh of relief and went back to bed. But the mouse came back and soon I gave up, turned the light back on, and read, with glasses held together by duct tape.

My morning walk the next day took me down toward the east end of the pond about a quarter of a mile away, where the home closest to my cabin stood at the edge of a marsh. Wood smoke curled up from the chimney of the tiny home. The roof was corrugated tin and the sides were a mix of weathered shingles and tar paper. As I wondered if anybody actually lived there year-round, the door opened.

"Come over here, young man, and let me get a look at you," said an ancient woman with a big potbelly.

I did as I was told, and when I reached her front stoop I realized how small she was. I'm only five foot seven, and the top of this woman's head barely cleared my waist. A cigarette dangled out the side of her mouth, and she looked me up and down as if inspecting a horse for purchase. I half expected her to check my teeth. Her dress, with a rip on the side, looked like it was made from faded curtains. But despite the wrinkles, the smoke, and the tattered clothes, there was something much more important—a twinkle in her eye. Whenever I see this rare sign of mirth, of human sparkle, I'm drawn to such a person like a moth to a flame.

"I'm Millie. Who are you?"

"I'm Mike."

"Well, Mike, come on in for coffee."

And just like that Millie and I became friends. Her one-room home was decorated with dice hanging from the ceiling and a deer's head mounted on the wall. The scent of wood smoke was mixed with a musty odor. I sat on a battered couch with more lumps than a prizefighter's face. We talked for half an hour, and though I mentioned I'd bought what Vermonters call a "camp," she never asked me which one. She was too busy describing how her little home was in a piece of heaven, and how she had become too old to spend the winters here alone but hated to go down to the "city," meaning Montpelier. I guessed Millie's age to be about eighty-five, and she said she'd been coming here for the last forty years.

Millie told me what I could expect to find in the pond, from giant snapping turtles to smallmouth bass. She confided she'd seen a moose amble by, but that no one believed her. (At that time, 1978, New England's moose population was relatively small compared to today, and most were in northern Maine.)

As I was leaving, she asked if I had met Herb.

"Who's Herb?"

"Herb's the black bear that wanders around here. It's a big one, so I figure it's a *he*. Emmet, down the road, says he followed

Herb's tracks this winter and they led up the ridge to the A-frame. Emmet thinks the bear likes to sleep under that cabin."

I didn't tell her it was my cabin. I felt faint, thinking I had just paid all this money and would never come up here again.

Should you think I'm the world's biggest chicken, here's what five other "outdoor lovers" wrote in the cabin guest book over the next couple of years:

*I am here alone and enjoying it, although last night when I had to return to the car, I carried two flashlights, a hatchet, a shovel, and the bass spear. I love a night in the forest.*

*I bumped into a black dog last night at 8:00 in the pitch dark and almost died.*

*Harry was terrified of noises last night. He swears he saw the lights go on and off, and a bear look in the window.*

*Conversations around the fire: Cogs talked of asteroids and superconductivity, Boomer talked of real estate and yachts, and Dale didn't really talk at all, just a question every 10 or 15 minutes, "What is that noise? Did you hear it? Sounded big."*

*I did not sleep the entire night: due to the fact that I kept thinking about the bear.*

CHAPTER 3

# RELUCTANT GUESTS, OUTHOUSES, AND A NEW CAREER

*So where do people go to the bathroom?*
—A PROSPECTIVE GUEST

I kept pictures of the cabin on my cubicle wall at work and gazed longingly at them, thinking of that first walk I had taken around the property in May, greeting the trees and getting to know the land. To this day, those little pictures have an instant calming effect, and when I'm overworked I often drive up to the cabin and spend a few days alone, decompressing. After that first solo visit, however, going to the cabin alone was not an option: I needed guests who would brave the nights with me.

Finding such victims, er . . . guests, proved more difficult than I expected. People loved Vermont, loved getting away for a weekend in the country, didn't they? I did my best to describe the pond in glowing terms, mentioning the chance to see abundant wildlife and the possibility of catching trophy-size trout from nearby rivers and smallmouth bass from the pond. Coworkers and friends would become enthused and ask to see a photograph of the cabin. After seeing the picture, they would pause, say that it looked cute, and start with the questions. Of course, I believed in full disclosure (as my realtor should have done), and the questions and answers went something like this:

17

"How many bedrooms does it have?"

"It sleeps eight."

"So, it's got a lot of bedrooms, huh?"

"Not exactly; it's got one."

"You mean one big bedroom and then some people sleep in the den?"

"Not exactly. The den and the bedroom are combined."

"Is the kitchen also in this one big room?"

"Yeah, but I've got some work to do in the kitchen area."

The prospective guest usually figured this was the catch—they were being recruited to do carpentry. Rather smugly they would say, "And you need my help, right?"

"No, no. I just want you to relax. I'm going to hire a professional at some point for the kitchen work. But first I need to have a well drilled."

This stopped them cold, the look of realization that there was no running water and no plumbing slowly spreading across their faces. The next question, to which no one wanted the answer, was invariably the same:

"So where do people go to the bathroom?"

I would anticipate their reaction and tried to diffuse it with a little history.

"They use the outhouse, the same way people have done for hundreds of thousands of years."

"Wow. Sounds like fun." Then they'd wander off, or take a rain check, or say something polite but noncommittal.

The aversion to using an outhouse struck me as rather odd, since it had never bothered me. The flushable toilet is a relatively new luxury, said to have been invented by Thomas Crapper in London, England. (He served as the Royal Sanitary Engineer. Surprisingly, he was never knighted, so he never became Sir Thomas and had to continue on as Mr. Crapper.) Anyway, using an outhouse goes back as far as eating, and we haven't stopped that, have we? And it wasn't as though my outhouse was a two-seater. (I always wondered if the occupants inside two-seaters were expected to talk and, if so, what they discussed. Just wondering.) I've even read about five-holers, complete with wood-stove. My outhouse, on the other hand, was totally private.

And the porcupine was even gone. That first weekend I had waited till it ventured out of its lair, then sealed the back of the outhouse with plywood. The displaced porcupine must have adjusted fine to life outside, because I never saw another one the rest of the summer.

In trying to convince prospective houseguests to visit, I did my outhouse research. I learned that firewood was often stacked along the path to the outhouse so that on the return trip, folks could bring in an armful and by evening have gathered enough wood to last the night. Outhouse doors should always face south and open inward. That way you can leave it open and enjoy the warmth of the sun but have access to it for quick closing. Some outhouses had a Dutch door, which made it possible for those on the outside to see the occupant's head, but not their lower half. Outhouses in one-room schools sometimes were attached to the schoolroom rather than set fifty yards out back. (That's where the term "fifty-yard dash" comes from.) Placing the outhouse inside the schoolroom was cruel and inhuman punishment for those with a functioning sense of smell, particularly in warm weather. I'm convinced this is the reason children across America have summers off today. One last outhouse fact for inquiring minds: 97 percent of American households have television sets, but only 94 percent have indoor plumbing. Despite this, the outhouse made my cabin a tough sell.

So I expanded my recruiting campaign to include all of my coworkers, distant cousins, and casual acquaintances. In the end I had three takers: Cogs, Boomer, and Dale—all friends from elementary school. Of the three, only two lasted more than one trip: Dale dropped out after the first outing due to a few ill-timed practical jokes we played on him.

That left Cogs and Boomer, who were as opposite as night and day. Cogs is a laid-back, six-foot-five-inch string bean, whose strength is diplomacy and tact. He also has the uncanny ability to shut out the outside world, sometimes including me, to preserve his "centeredness." He is a true product of the sixties and keeps an open mind on all things, leaning toward the liberal side of most issues, and always presenting his case in a thoughtful, sensitive way. Boomer, on the other hand, is the proverbial bull in a china shop, never afraid to follow his first hunch. (He recently told me he felt like he was getting in a rut living in Boston, and within two weeks had moved to Hong Kong.) Boomer often misses the subtleties, yet he's one of the most open and honest people I know and quick to apologize when he's at fault. And Cogs and I often feel he is at fault.

Sometimes a fog seems to surround Boomer, making him dangerous to be with. On a recent canoeing trip, Boomer's job was to secure the canoe to the top of the car while I loaded up the fishing gear. The fog must have descended, because he never got the job done and was waiting for me in the front seat. I assumed all was ready and off we went, zipping along until we came to the first traffic light. When I stepped on the brakes, the canoe shot forward like a missile, hitting a passing car broadside. The occupants were fine, but dazed, wondering how they had come to be waylaid by a canoe.

Later, Boomer casually mentioned that next time I should drive more carefully.

Boomer, Cogs, and Dale were my first real guests to the cabin after my brother Bob's April visit. I believe they came for three reasons: curiosity about my investment, the great fishing in northern Vermont, and pity. I was ecstatic to have company and was fairly honest with them; I explained about the porcupine and the outhouse, the cabin's rough shape, and I even told them about Herb, the bear. (I didn't mention this to Dale, because even during our backyard campouts he had asked a lot of questions about bears.)

One additional glitch greeted my guests, but at that time even I didn't know about it. It only happens from May 15 to June 15, peaking in the middle of this period. We arrived on May 30.

Since my driveway was full of deep ruts from spring runoff, we had to leave Cogs's car at the base of the hill, by Millie's home. Millie was in her garden, and from a distance it looked like she had a wedding veil over her head. When I felt that first sharp, painful bite on my arm, I realized she was covered in a head net. Within seconds of getting out of the car, hordes of bloodthirsty winged devils were upon us. It was May 30—the dead middle of blackfly season.

For those of you who have not had the pleasure of meeting the blackfly, allow me to introduce you to the bane of the North Woods. Particularly vexing to the tourist industry, they make a short season even shorter. Think about it. After the bitter winter comes the drabness of mud season. Then, just as the land awakens and folks are teased by occasional warmth, out come the blackflies. Unlike the mosquito, which breeds in the standing water of swamps, blackflies originate from streams and rivers, which are found all over northern New England. They seek out warm-blooded creatures and attack in swarms that even Alfred Hitchcock couldn't imagine. As Millie later said, "Those bugs can drive you to distraction." Cogs's guest book entry was equally accurate when he wrote, *Bring BloodMobile for visits in late May.*

We hoofed it up the hill, toting our gear and swatting the flies, with Boomer muttering something about knowing what it felt like to carry Bwana's luggage on safari.

On my last trip the night had brought terror with thoughts of the bear; however, this time it brought comfort. As soon as the sun went down, the blackflies vanished and we were free to sit out by the campfire in front of the cabin. We made plans to fish the river, and set two alarms to wake us at 4:00 A.M. All of us were avid anglers, having fished together since we were old enough to ride our bikes down to the Connecticut River near our homes in suburban Longmeadow.

When the alarms went off, there was a lot of moaning and groaning and no one made a move to shut them off, but instead burrowed deeper into their sleeping bags. Finally, I got up and turned on the lights and shut off the alarms. I looked at the three bodies curled up in their sleeping bags and shouted for them to get up. Cogs replied, "Shut up and turn the lights off." I left the lights on and went around shaking the crew. Boomer sat up and muttered that since he was awake he might as well get up. He then ripped a long fart that made Cogs and Dale slide deeper into their sleeping bags.

Boomer boiled water for instant coffee and I put out some sad-looking store-bought coffee cake. Once Boomer and I had poured our coffee and started eating, Cogs and Dale emerged from their bags. They got up not just for the hot coffee and cake, but because they knew Boomer and I were really going to drive down to the river, and neither wanted to miss the chance at a lunker brown trout. At that time in our lives our angling objective had nothing to do with communing with nature and everything to do with competition.

To save time we decided to finish our coffee and cake in the car while we drove the twenty minutes to the river. Cogs drove and I sat in the front, feeling a bit like a burglar to be driving at such an odd hour. When we passed the outskirts of a small farm, I was amazed at the number of deer by the side of the road illuminated by our headlights. In a two-mile stretch just north of Montpelier we saw nine deer. They were feeding on the grass alongside the road, and when the headlights cut through the foggy darkness, the deer would stare at the car for a moment, then leap into the darkness after we were about fifteen feet away.

Arriving at the river at 4:30 A.M., we were surprised that it was still pitch black. Cogs dropped each one of us at a different stretch of river. I won't soon forget the next thirty minutes, sitting by its swollen waters in the dark, waiting for the gray of dawn to see enough to cast my line. The bone-chilling dampness spread throughout my body, leaving me in a torpid state. Finally, when I could see a bit, I waded into the river, and a shadow the size of a small submarine glided away from the shallows. It was the biggest trout I had ever seen, no doubt a brown trout foraging along the bank to ambush a minnow. Big browns need large meals, and as they grow, their diet evolves from insects to larger aquatic creatures such as minnows and crayfish. Really big browns will even eat mice or small snakes that fall or otherwise venture into the water.

On my second cast, one of those monsters actually hit my

weighted Muddler Minnow with a strike that jarred me. It broke off in two seconds, but that small glimpse was enough to give me the fever to fish for giant browns for years to come. The rest of the outing was slow, and I caught only one small brook trout and one rainbow trout. The others had about the same kind of luck, but Boomer confirmed that he'd seen an enormous brown at first light. When I asked him where, he said "at a secret spot."

We left the river about 9:00 A.M. for a hearty breakfast back at the cabin. Cogs showed his culinary skills by frying up eggs and bacon over an open fire, while Boomer and I offered encouragement as we drank cup after cup of coffee. Most likely, we missed the best fishing because while the sun may have prompted the brown trout to head for deeper water, the warming air probably increased the trout's metabolism. Even a rise in water temperature of two or three degrees will help put sluggish trout in a feeding mood.

After breakfast my guests helped me insulate and panel the walls of the cabin, one of the few home repairs I had set out to do. By afternoon we were hot and exhausted and headed down to the pond. We all dove in except Dale, who couldn't swim a stroke. Instead, he decided to float on a massive air mattress and, using a mask and snorkel, hung his head over the front to see what aquatic life lurked below. (He probably needed a diversion from thinking about Herb, because at the tail end of the campfire party, I had spilled the beans and told the complete story, in a lighthearted mood. Dale didn't sleep a wink all night and had to listen to us snore while he tried to take his mind off bears.)

Boomer and I had recovered from the shock of the cold water and were doing a little snorkeling of our own when I got the bright idea to scare Dale. Boomer encouraged me, saying my scheme showed bold and original thinking, and together we reversed direction and slowly made our way toward Dale. When we were within twenty feet, I put the plan into motion. Boomer's role was to watch, enjoy, and record what transpired for posterity. I took a large breath of air and slipped beneath the surface, swimming under Dale's raft, where I spotted his head. He was looking straight down through the mask into the weeds. I then darted over so that my head now came face to face with his. Looking up at him, I saw the terror in his eyes as he recoiled from a human head popping up from the weeds, just inches from his face. Boomer later told me how Dale's scream echoed off the mountains and how he paddled the raft so hard it looked like it was motorized.

Had I spent more time showing Dale the things I loved about the pond and less time on pranks, I might have kept him as a regular guest. But when I was in my twenties, long-term thinking was not one of my stronger virtues.

Two other noteworthy incidents occurred on the pond that afternoon, both involving Boomer and both involving fishing equipment. From experience, I had always made him sit in the front of the canoe, figuring at least I could watch him and possibly have a second or two notice when his personal fog rolled in and the trouble started. The combination of canoes and Boomer doesn't bode well for me. Not just because of the flying canoe incident, but because of other times when he seems to forget he is on the water altogether. Sometimes he lurches to one side or stands up to cast, but the worst dunking I ever took was just a few feet from shore. At the very end of a day on a lake, things had gone so well I let my guard down. As we headed back to the launching site, he swung a leg out of the canoe about ten feet from shore, thinking he could stand in shallow water. While it may have looked a foot deep, it was more like six feet. When Boomer went to stand, he pitched over wildly, taking the canoe and me with him. *Just ten more feet . . .*

So this day I was trying to keep one eye on him and the other on the tip of my rod as we trolled for bass. However, his mind was on trout, and he talked about being back on the river tomorrow, arranging his tackle as we cruised the pond. He pulled out a two-inch silver Rapala Minnow and rhetorically asked if it was a floater or a sinker. I looked just in time to see him put it over the side of the canoe for a test. It was a sinker, because before he could grab the lure, down it went, lost for good. I couldn't help but laugh, telling him he had discovered a foolproof testing procedure.

Things settled down after that and Boomer focused on the bass. Each of us caught two twelve-inch smallmouths. We were competing as usual, and with fifteen minutes left in our mindless derby I decided to switch flies. In that moment of concentrated knot tying, Boomer hauled back with his spinning rod for a mighty cast. His lure apparently hooked the end of my rod, and when he cast his line it took my rod right out of my lap and into the water. The L.L. Bean special sank in a slow and sickening way, spiraling to the depths of the pond.

We both sat in shocked silence. Since it was an accident, I bit my tongue. I wished Boomer had done the same. Instead he offered words of condolence. "Sorry, but don't feel bad. Remember, some of my stuff is down there too."

"Some of your stuff!" I screamed. "You've got one little Rapala lure at the bottom of the pond, and I've got an entire rod and reel!"

"Calm down, calm down," he answered. "It's time to head in; cocktail hour awaits and tomorrow's a new day."

When the alarm went off the next morning, I went to the outhouse, shocked at how cold the air had turned. We all decided it was too cold for trout, except Boomer, who said he'd give it a try. So while we went back to bed, Boomer drove down to the river.

Later, after lunch, we began to worry when he still hadn't returned. For all we knew he could be at the bottom of the river. Falling into water with a pair of old-fashioned hip or chest waders had claimed the lives of more than one angler. The waders immediately fill up with water, carrying the victim to the bottom before he has time to take them off. The water-filled waders act like the cement galoshes the Mafia uses on stool pigeons, but in the case of anglers, the sinking is accidental—usually a result of not paying attention to your surroundings. Boomer was particularly good at this. I had a chilling picture of him standing on the river bottom, fishing for all eternity.

We needn't have worried. He stayed on the river until late in the day, when the sun warmed the water as well as the metabolism of the fish. He came back with a smile, toting something huge in the cooler, and immediately made his entry into the guest book:

*Well, my 22-inch brown trout should hold the record for many years to come. Caught it at three o'clock. Mike and I will stop at the river on the way home tomorrow so I can give him some pointers. I'll write of this experience next trip. Until then—Boomer.*

Before I left that weekend, I read the half-dozen entries in the guest book and realized it revealed how we were learning the ways of the trout. Two of the entries mentioned that the only trout caught were at the bottom of the river during high water, and another said that the trout didn't start biting in early spring until at least noontime. I began to see how I could use the entries and what I had learned during my time on the river to write an article. My brother Mark had recently sold a piece about his travels in Italy to a local newspaper, and I had been thinking of doing the same.

That night, when I returned home, I wrote the draft of a story about fishing in Vermont, with suggestions for working the rivers when the water was cold and high. It was crude, with short, stilted sentences and very basic advice. I sent it out anyway, and three weeks later received a note from a newspaper asking if I had any photographs to go with it. I couldn't believe they were really going to run it! I sent them not just one photo, but twenty. A week later the story ran; they mailed me a copy with a check for a whopping fifteen dollars. Seeing that little article turned on a switch somewhere deep inside me. The minuscule check represented something much more important than the bigger checks I had earned in my working world. The article was a tangible product, the direct result of something I had worked on from start to finish. Best of all, I could actually hold that product in my hand. This little article gave me a sense of satisfaction I wanted more of.

Over the next three months I made it my mission to write more articles. Most were rejected, but there were a couple of successes, such as a lengthy piece in *Trout* magazine and another in *Outdoor Life*. There were even words of encouragement to keep me going. I learned that even in rejection there can be encouragement, such as that I received from premier fly-fishing editor and writer Nick Lyons. The rejection letter from his publishing house was the typical form letter, but on the bottom in ink was scrawled, "I like your writing, stay with it. Nick Lyons."

That's all I needed. A new moonlighting career was launched, and I would mine my material from the rivers by the cabin. But first I had to learn to be a little more comfortable in the woods: It wouldn't look good for an outdoor writer to be too chicken to stay alone at his own cabin. It was time to be brave and start coming here solo.

The guest book entries from that first spring tell a tale of the cabin's comforts:

*Arrived at noon and have been carrying supplies up the hill ever since. Mike, please install gondola.*

*After reading this guest book over I have concluded that the cabin has seen many good times. All trips have been recorded except the ones where manual dexterity did not permit it (30-degree temperatures).*

*After riding in the car for four hours with the radio on, the shock of arriving to total silence in the dark is enough to unnerve anybody, let alone a city-dweller.*

*There's nothing like an outhouse to bring on constipation.*

# CHAPTER 4

# MEETING THE NEIGHBORS

*Nature teaches more than she preaches.*
*There are no sermons in stones.*
—JOHN BURROUGHS

Each trip that first summer yielded some new insight into both the wildlife sharing my hilltop and the neighbors. I use the term "neighbors" rather loosely, because no homes or cabins can be seen from my A-frame, which is walled in by woods on three sides, while on the fourth is a view over the pond toward a mountain range. The nearest people lived a quarter mile away at the base of my ridge, where Millie's home and two other small homes were located. Having my cabin high up on the hilltop was a real benefit, because it felt like being in a wilderness, hundreds of miles from other people.

Most of the people who lived nearby were of French Canadian heritage and went out of their way to help me, such as offering tips for fishing spots and pushing my car out of mud. The men and women liked their cigarettes, beer, and whiskey, and both were jacks-of-all-trades. While I couldn't hammer a nail straight, many of them had built their homes from salvaged materials—the lumber, wiring, plumbing, and everything else. The men operated chainsaws as though they had been doing it since childhood— and they probably had. Many had "deer camps" way back in the hills that they used during the hunting season. I thought this was strange; their houses were on dirt roads in the woods, yet they needed camps even farther out in the woods. I suspect the camps were as much for having a week away with the boys as they were for deer hunting.

To a suburbanite flatlander like myself, the locals had some peculiarities; for instance, their penchant for burning. If a branch fell on their lawn, they'd burn it in the yard rather than drag it to the woods. And every third house seemed to have a tag sale going at all times. At one, I took notice of the offerings: a giant bra, two stuffed animals, and a rolling pin. Many of the area's homes had bug zappers that stayed on around the clock during the summer, killing many more beneficial insects than mosquitoes. Used tires were sometimes rolled down the hill "out back" to rest alongside the broken fridge and stove.

The stories I could tell about the locals would probably pale in comparison to what they thought of me—especially after I bought a used bicycle. A woman living near Millie had two bikes for sale. While one had rusted into some kind of modern sculpture, the other wasn't too bad.

"I can give you a good deal on the good one, make your daughter real happy," she said.

"It's for me."

"Oh. You want *that* one?" She paused, giving me the once-over, then quickly said, "It's yours for ten dollars."

"Will you take eight? I need gas money to get home."

"Sold."

And so I was the proud owner of a used bike. There was just one problem: It was a girl's bike, and it was pink. But hey, at eight dollars it was a bargain.

I wanted a bike to cruise the dirt roads that crisscrossed the region, thinking I could enjoy the flora and fauna I might miss while driving. While out for my first ride, I found some wild daisies that I thought would brighten up the cabin. I picked them and circled the pond on my used pink bike. During my stays at the cabin, I usually wore my oldest clothes, and on that day I happened to be wearing a Hawaiian shirt from my college days and a pair of powder blue polyester pants, which Cogs said looked like they were inflatable. My hunch is that the folks who saw me pedal by wondered just what kind of flatlander had bought the A-frame on the ridge.

While the bike never got me into any serious trouble, an incident occurred that first summer that almost did. It happened at a tiny restaurant fifteen miles to the north where I'd struck up a friendship with two waitresses. Business always seemed to be slow, so Boomer, Cogs, and I often had the place to ourselves. The jukebox was loaded with classics like "Beer Barrel Polka," and "I Let a Wino Decorate My Living Room." Well, one morning, things were particularly slow and the music was right, so I decided to dance—and soon the waitresses and my buddies joined in. We had worked up to a slow song—Elvis's "Love Me Tender"— when the other patrons ambled in and did a double take at the local girls dancing with the flatlanders at eight in the morning. Under their cold stares we returned to our eggs and hash browns.

A year later when I returned to the diner, this time with a girlfriend, both waitresses were gone and an older woman was running the show. When she approached our table, I was prepared to give our order, but she spoke first.

"This ain't no dance hall," she said flatly, hands on her hips.

"Pardon me?" I said.

"I heard about the comin's and goin's-on while you were here last year, and there ain't gonna be any more of that."

It was a long ride back to the cabin. After I tried to explain to my girlfriend, I kept wondering how the woman knew me. How could she have recognized me a year later, especially when she hadn't even been there? I never did figure that out, but I suspect we were the talk of the town. In addition to my ever more rigorous mountain-man training, I clearly had a lot to learn about small-town living.

So I slowly got to know my neighbors and they, me. I also was learning to identify more trees, plants, and flowers, such as the painted trillium, with its white flower and crimson center, that graced the forest floor in the springtime. From a distance the flowering trillium looked like individual snowflakes dappling the brown forest floor. And along the pond, wild iris, called Slender Blue Flag, grew two feet high, crowned with the most delicate purple flowers. My eye was becoming attuned to these colors amid the predominant greens, browns, and blue of the pond and woods, and I'd spend hours floating in my canoe with a field guide identifying the wetland plants. It seemed I had never seen yellows as vivid as the floating flower of the pond lilies, or violets as bright as the flowering spikes on the pickerelweed.

I discovered which streams had brook trout and which had browns. I could distinguish the hum of the mosquito from the subtle drone of the blackfly without opening my eyes. The more I learned about my environment, the more confidence I felt. Nothing, however, prepared me for my first encounter with the bear.

It was a late September afternoon of my first year at the cabin. I was in the habit of exploring the old logging roads that spread out like capillaries from the pond road. After hiking the hills opposite the pond, I stopped to rest above a logging field. Just below me, about eighty feet away, a movement in the field caught my eye.

With powerful paws a large black bear was turning over logs and lowering its head to lick up the larvae, ants, and grubs. The bear was so engaged it never saw me on the hill, nor, since I was downwind, did it catch my scent. A bear's eyesight is poor, more attuned to movement than color, so if a person is still, the bear can remain unaware of his or her presence. They usually rely on their keen sense of smell and hearing to warn them that people are nearby.

Surprisingly, while I was a little startled, I wasn't really afraid. But I was awed by this incredible opportunity to witness such an elusive wild animal. Normally nocturnal, most black bears stay close to dense cover in the daytime, yet this one was clearly visible and at least a hundred feet from the edge of the forest. I knew I might never get another chance to see one so near, so I studied it closely, noting its rounded ears, long muzzle, and stubby tail. I had plenty of time to observe the huge but harmless-looking animal quietly feeding and turning over large logs with ease, in a methodical, unhurried way.

I watched the bear for twenty minutes, until light began to fade. To return to the cabin I had to climb down the ridge and pass by the edge of the old logging field—and the bear. Better to let the bear see me now rather than startle it as I passed by, especially as darkness grew closer. I decided to clap my hands.

Immediately the bear stood on its hind legs, trying to pinpoint the sound. It no longer appeared harmless. Its head was enormous, looking bigger than a basketball and almost as wide as its shoulders. I figure it weighed about four hundred pounds, and in the standing position must have been almost eight feet tall.

It seemed vexed that it could not locate the sound of the clap. Staying on its hind feet, the bear kept sticking its nose up in the air for a whiff of whatever had interrupted its feeding. The light had dimmed, and my adrenaline surged as I wondered what to do next.

I shouted. The bear dropped to all fours and hit the ground running, barreling through the logging field like a runaway freight train. It headed away from me, right down the path toward the cabin.

*OK*, I said to myself, *now it's almost dark and there's an angry bear who didn't get to finish its meal somewhere between me and the cabin. Or at the cabin. Didn't Millie say one slept beneath it?*

I had to get off that hill fast, while I could still see a few feet in front of me. I picked up a stick and started walking, then realized a stick was worthless against a four-hundred-pound bear. I had to try a different tact. And so I sang. I sang some of the same tunes I had danced to at the breakfast place: a little Elvis, a little "Beer Barrel Polka." I sang loud. I wanted the bear to know exactly where I was—the thought of surprising it in the dark was too horrifying to consider.

The mile walk back to the cabin in twilight was more than a little creepy. Except for an occasional birdcall and the crunching of fallen leaves under my boots, the woods were silent. I wondered if the bear was ahead somewhere off the side of the path, listening to my approaching footsteps. Bears do not like to be cornered, and I hoped my singing would have a calming effect. When I reached the dirt road along the edge of the pond I began to relax a little, but kept singing until I reached the cabin. I sat out on the porch and poured myself a large glass of peppermint schnapps. Whether it was the effects of the schnapps or the adrenaline wearing off, I began to see how ridiculous it was to worry about this bear. It could have mauled me on that hill, but instead it ran away. And it didn't live under the cabin—I know, because I forced myself to look with a flashlight.

I read my tracking book, and sure enough it said that most black bears avoid people and display aggressiveness only when protecting their cubs. The trouble starts when people start giving them handouts of food. Then the bear associates people with food, and the animal's native fear of people is replaced by stubbornness. The worst problems are when bears visit campsites to forage for food. I have a friend who spent one of the longest nights of his life at a remote campsite in Maine where a black bear repeatedly approached the tent trying to get food. It finally found the cooler outside the tent, ripped it to shreds, and ate the contents. That still wasn't enough. For the next six hours the bear snorted and kept getting closer to the tent. Even when my friend forced himself out of the tent and built a raging fire, the bear retreated just a few feet away.

I figured I would avoid that problem by never throwing food scraps in the woods or leaving any garbage outside the cabin. Then the bear would stick to natural food—nuts, acorns, berries, insects, mice, reptiles, and carrion. I also read in my book that bears will stay away from people as long as they can find adequate food in the wild, and we can assist them by protecting their habitat. They prefer mixed stands of hardwoods and softwoods, usually near swamps, and lakes or rivers edged with brushy undergrowth. I was a bit disturbed to see that although bears may shuffle along at a slow gait, they are capable of short bursts of speed up to thirty-two miles an hour. Expert tree climbers, they will sometimes climb a tree for honey or nuts—even stacking up broken branches to make a platform for resting, what sometimes are called "bear nests." This is often done in beech trees, where they spend considerable amounts of time in the fall, gathering beechnuts.

I made a mental note to leave the beech trees on my property unharmed to provide the bear plenty of natural food.

Alone on the porch I began realizing how seldom I sat quietly letting thoughts flow unencumbered without the constant stimuli around. And I thought about what was in my hand: the glass of schnapps. I realized I was drinking more than I should. Gradually my lifestyle had fallen into a pattern of excessive drinking every weekend. That night I glimpsed into the future, and I didn't like what I saw. I was following the crowd of young corporate climbers, but I wasn't happy. I didn't want to end up as a sixty-year-old with heart problems who drank to dull the pain of what might have been. Here on the mountain I had moments of true joy, feeling a sense of well-being without worrying about fitting in or conforming. The little natural things inspired me to stop and appreciate their simplicity and the pleasure they brought. I found satisfaction in what the seasons offered, such as the cheerful sound of peepers in the spring, a languid swim in the pond on a hot summer day, or simply watching a red maple leaf floating down a stream in autumn. It was at that moment I decided to change the path I was on. If I wanted to channel more of my energy into my writing and learning, I would need to be clearheaded on the weekends.

Thoreau went to the woods to live more deliberately. I now went to the woods to change my life too. I figured if I could come up to the cabin alone more often, I could explore and learn more about my surroundings by day and write at night. It would be the perfect match—the woods would be my classroom and the cabin would be my workshop. There was so much to learn. I loved the outdoors but didn't understand most of the connections taking place around me every minute. To comprehend the subtleties of nature, I would have to quiet myself and not try to rush the learning process. All of us have the power to observe more, understand more, and appreciate more, but that comes about through an inner stillness—something I was just beginning to develop.

A light rain began falling, and I listened to the rhythmic sound of its drops pattering on the leaves. It would have been heaven to sleep on the porch that night, but my comfort level with the forest still forced me inside, behind my locked door.

The next morning dawned with a hint of humidity in the air instead of the crisp days one might expect in Vermont in September. Rather than hike, I decided to spend the day at the pond swimming and fishing. I was now in the habit of taking an early morning skinny-dip, which not only woke me up, but also made me feel like a kid again. I lay on the little dock I had built and looked down into the clear water. On the bottom of the pond what looked like a rock started to move. It was a snapping turtle with a shell about two feet across. I thought twice about getting in the water without a bathing suit.

The snapper's massive head and knobby shell were masked with algae and looked prehistoric. Its back end was buried in the mud, perhaps to better ambush a passing fish. Although these turtles look slow, they can strike with extreme speed. I had read that snappers feed on aquatic plants, small mammals, and invertebrates, sometimes even grabbing a small bird that has fallen into the water. I have yet to hear of a snapper in the water bothering a human; they usually just drift off to deeper water when disturbed. However, snappers on land will defend themselves because they feel vulnerable out of the water. Some people are concerned when they spot a large snapping turtle in their lake or pond, but the turtle is actually helping the water stay clean by eating carrion. They're easiest to spot in June, when they emerge from the water to lay eggs in sand or gravel.

I watched the turtle beneath the dock for several minutes, reminding myself to take a quick look before I stepped into the water for my next swim.

After getting dressed again, I decided to do some fishing at a spot where the road runs parallel to the water's edge. A twelve-year-old boy was wading in the water and suddenly caught the largest bullfrog I've ever seen, as big as my hiking boot. I was beginning to think everything grows to enormous size in my pond, except the fish.

With a big smile on his face, the boy brought the bullfrog over to show me.

"That's one heck of a bullfrog," I said.

"Yep, never got one like this before. It's bigger than most of the fish I catch."

"Me too. What are you going to do with it?"

"Not sure. Maybe keep it for a pet."

"You ought to let it go; it lives here."

"I guess. But he'd be safe with me."

"Don't you worry about that frog," I said, "he's so big there isn't a bass in the pond large enough to eat him."

"Well, I guess you're right, but I sure would like to keep him."

"How about I take your picture with him and give it to you next time I come up? That way you could show the picture to everyone and still let him go. I do that with most of the big fish I catch."

I took my camera out of my pack, took the boy's picture holding the frog, and he released it into the pond. Then I moved back to my fishing spot and the boy to his. After working my way up and down the shoreline, I ended up with only one pickerel to show for my efforts.

Suddenly I heard a scream. I ran toward the boy, thinking he'd gotten a hook stuck in his hand. As I approached, he was pointing into the pond, jumping up and down.

"That snake's got my bullfrog!"

I couldn't believe my eyes. A two-foot-long brown snake had the leg of the bullfrog down his throat. The snake was swimming parallel to the shoreline, just seven or eight feet off, with the boy following along. Although the snake's head was dwarfed by the bullfrog, somehow the snake was in control.

I ripped my backpack off and grabbed my camera, zooming in on this life-and-death scene. As I shot frame after frame, the snake glided to within three feet of the shore. Occasionally the snake would twist around and the bullfrog would roll with it. The snake would quickly open its mouth wider, trying to get a better grip.

"Mister, aren't you going to save my frog?" the boy hollered, his eyes enormous.

I stopped taking pictures, looked at the boy, then back to the drama between the snake and the bullfrog. The bullfrog wasn't even struggling; it seemed resigned to its fate.

"I don't think your bullfrog's going to make it."

"We gotta try! You're the one who told me to let it go; you said it would be safe, that nothing would eat it."

"I hadn't thought of a snake. I've never seen anything like this."

"Then do something!" he shouted.

I tried to reason with him. "But this is nature; the snake is just trying to get its dinner."

The boy hung his head with disappointment, and I went back to photographing the event.

"You've got to kill that snake!" he screamed.

I looked at the boy, not knowing what to do.

The snake had now moved within a foot of shore and seemed to be in a standoff with the bullfrog. I had the feeling that the snake would take all day to get the bullfrog completely in his mouth and down his throat. It was repulsive yet fascinating, and I knew I was witnessing one of the everyday struggles of the natural world.

The snake and frog thrashed wildly, and I leaned over the water to within a foot of them to capture the perfect wildlife photo. Then the water exploded in a silver spray.

The boy had taken matters into his own hands and had thrown a huge rock at the snake. It coughed out the leg like a person would spit out a watermelon seed and then slithered off, hiding in the brush along the shore.

Within five minutes the snake was swimming back to where the bullfrog floated half alive in the lily pads. The boy had been keeping an eye on "his" bullfrog and screamed to me again.

"It's coming back!"

I ran over. This was one aggressive snake. I thought of the poisonous snakes in the area and ruled out rattlesnake, but thought maybe this was a copperhead. The notion that this snake was in "my" pond didn't appeal to me.

The boy said, "Please, mister, kill that snake; it's no good."

I picked up a five-foot-long stick, waited until the snake was within striking distance, and slammed the stick into its midsection. The snake writhed in pain and I hit it again—this time in the head—killing it instantly.

The boy treated me like a hero. But I wasn't particularly pleased with myself, especially when I got back to the cabin and looked up the snake in my field guide. It was a nonpoisonous water snake. I had let pressure from the boy, and my misunderstanding of snakes, get the better of me. I was looking at the natural world in human terms, trying to protect the weak from the strong, instead of trying to understand the natural order of predator and prey. The snake was just doing what it had to do to survive. Just as the bullfrog ate bugs, the snake ate bullfrogs, and a hawk or great blue heron would undoubtedly eat the snake. I had learned a new lesson about life in the natural world. There are no good and bad creatures, and from now on I was going to live and let live with all my neighbors.

My guest book entry for that week hinted at the lesson I had learned:

*Another great visit to the cabin—except for when I made the mistake of killing a snake that had a captured a bullfrog . . .*

# CHAPTER 5

# CLOSE ENCOUNTERS: THE BIG IMPACT OF SMALL CREATURES

*We found everywhere an abundance of wild beasts*
*of all sorts, through this vast forest.*
—DANIEL BOONE

Each summer evening, right on schedule the bats appeared in the clearing, like mice with wings, swooping low to catch mosquitoes. During the summer of my second year at the cabin, I would sit on the porch and sometimes throw a rock high into the clearing to see if they'd swoop for it; they always did.

Like snakes, bats have been given a bad rap by humans. Maybe out of my guilt for killing the snake, I watched the bats with respect and curiosity rather than revulsion. They were serving a useful purpose by keeping the insects under control, capturing their food in flight. The bats I was watching were probably Little Brown Myotis, which have a blunt nose, small teeth, and beady black eyes. They are about three-and-a-half inches long, but weigh only a quarter of an ounce. The winged membrane stretches from the front legs to the back legs, attaching to the foot. They catch insects in their wings, transferring them to their mouths in a split second. Like the snake, which is both predator and prey, the Little Brown bat is dinner for owls, common grackles, red-winged blackbirds, hawks, mink, and raccoons. Largemouth bass have even been known to grab a bat that lands on the water.

I always wondered how bats were able to catch something as small as a moving mosquito, and in *Wild Mammals of New England,* Alfred Godin gives the best explanation I've come across. He explains that flying bats emit rapid cries that increase as they near an object, judging distance by the time delay between the outgoing cry and the returning echo. The bat has a minute ear muscle that closes as the sound is emitted, which prevents it from hearing its own cry. The time delay for an object six inches from its mouth is an echo of about a thousandth of a second, giving the bat enough time to pinpoint a mosquito.

Bats were all around me at the cabin, and I enjoyed watching them in the twilight, especially since they kept to the clearing, about twenty feet from my seat on the porch. Some of them were braver, like the one that flew out of the outhouse as I was going in, prompting me to nickname it the "bat room." During my second summer, there was also one bat that swooped a little too close for comfort when I was fishing with Boomer. Apparently the bat confused our jitterbug lure, hanging from the rod, for the real thing and dove for it, pulling up short just before it would have hit Boomer in the face. It was a tender moment watching him panic.

"Oh God, that thing almost hit me! Did you see it?"

"See what?" I said.

"The bat, you idiot—it dive-bombed me. Let's get out of here. Can't you see there's a bunch of them out now that the sun's down?"

"OK, OK, let's go."

Boomer was in the bow of the canoe, paddling furiously. I pitched in with a couple of strokes, then picked up my rod and swung my lure just above Boomer's red hair. Sure enough another bat swooped down within inches of his head.

He screamed. "That one was so close I could hear its wings. Why are they coming after me? Don't stop paddling."

I paddled some more, then quietly picked up the fishing net. At the moment I let the netting touch the top of Boomer's head, I hollered, "There's one in your hair!"

Boomer dropped his paddle in mid-stroke and, using both hands, started hitting the top of his head. I was laughing so hard no sound came out, but when it did, it echoed off the mountains. Boomer was not pleased.

"You jerk," he said.

"Sorry, I couldn't help myself."

"I'll get you for this; we could have tipped over and lost all our stuff."

"You've already lost most of my stuff over the last two years, and you've been 'getting' me since second grade."

"Well, I'm still going to get you for this. You know how I hate the thought of something in my hair—you do too. Remember the owl that almost got you?"

It happened earlier that same summer when Boomer and I were at the cabin after I had just bought a game call. The little wooden whistle was supposed to imitate the sound of a wounded rabbit and call in predators, such as a coyote or a fox. At the time, coyotes were relatively rare in the area, and I had yet to see one. So we had the idea of calling one in. We walked to a clearing, sat by a tree, and blew the game call.

The directions said to blow once loudly and once softly, then wait for five minutes. A sharp blast on the whistle made a high-pitched scream, sending a shiver down my spine. The softer blow sounded like a rabbit on its last legs. Then we waited. Boomer was to keep watch on the edge of the field to the right, and I would do the same to the left. I thought we had a decent chance to lure in a coyote; it was dusk, there was no breeze, and I was quite proud of my calling ability. (I had practiced in the car on the way up until Boomer threatened to push the whistle down my throat.)

Nothing stirred in the woods. I kept a careful watch on the tree line, knowing the coyote would venture cautiously into the open. The one place I wasn't looking was directly behind me.

Five minutes went by and I figured I'd give another short blast. As soon as the scream sounded, I saw a dark object swooping toward me out of the corner of my eye. I ducked and turned my head just in time to see an alarmingly large owl pulling up a couple of feet from my face before banking hard and gliding back into the woods.

I knew by its brown coloring and two-foot length it was a great horned owl. And I had read that such birds are big enough to carry off a skunk. Add that to the list of animals I feared and another lesson I reluctantly learned in my outdoor education.

Boomer was almost as terrified as I was. "Put that stupid thing away, and let's go."

I was shaking, but I moved in a hurry. I haven't used the predator call since, nor have I tried to trick wildlife.

One August night during that second summer of owning the cabin, I went to bed as a lightning storm was building. By 1:00 A.M. the thunder was not so distant. I turned off the lights in the cabin and was lying on top of my sleeping bag. Lightning bolts flashed in the night sky and thunder echoed off the mountains. As the storm approached, the thunder turned into sharp cracks, sounding as if the storm was right overhead. I figured it was at its peak, and with each passing minute I realized the significance of the cabin's exposed location high on top of the hill. I was experiencing a storm like never before.

The saying about determining the distance of a lightning bolt by counting the seconds between the flash of lightning and the thunder had little meaning that night; the flash and the boom came at the same time. One crash was so loud the whole cabin shook like it had exploded. Grabbing the inner tube we use to float on the pond, I threw it on the cabin floor and hopped on to wait out the storm. I wanted every inch of my body to be touching rubber in case the cabin was hit. As bad as the thunder's crashes were, the lulls between bright streaks of lightning were worse. I was waiting in anticipation of the next hit. Not knowing when or where it would strike added a new dimension of anxiety for me. I clung to the inner tube as though I were being swept down a raging river. . . . It was my only hope of survival. I cursed the cabin for its location, its A-frame roof for adding even more height, and myself for being alone. Solitude is great when things are going well, but give me a friend when nature shows its anger.

After the thunderclaps receded to the east, rain fell steadily, drumming the roof and soothing my shattered nerves. I drifted off to sleep only to be awakened a couple of hours later by a rustling sound. Mice. I don't like mice. While I can appreciate the purpose of bats, mice give me the creeps, especially when they come out in the dark in full force. That night it seemed like there were armies of mice arriving in a steady stream.

I no longer wondered how they got into my cabin, which was tightly shut, as the white-footed mouse is a very clever adversary, capable of squeezing its body through openings no wider than a quarter of an inch. They can contaminate food, gnaw through utility wires, chew holes in clothing, walls, and almost anything while leaving droppings everywhere. One pair of adult mice is capable of having twenty-eight young in a year. It seemed like the whole family was here on the second floor, running as if playing a soccer game.

Because of my vow to learn all I could, I forced myself to read about mice. Acorns are the primary food source of white-footed mice, and the availability of acorns influences the mouse population from year to year. Mice also perform a great service for the forest by eating gypsy moth caterpillars, those aliens from Europe and Asia that threaten our oak forests. When the mouse population rises, the gypsy moth population declines. Besides the white-footed mice, the woods of Vermont also have similar-looking deer mice. They are roughly the same size, but can be distinguished by the color of their fur: The deer mouse is gray, and the white-footed mouse is brown with white feet. The white-footed mouse prefers to live among hemlocks and white pines, like those around my cabin, while the deer mouse is more often found in spruce and fir forests. Both are primary food sources for weasels, mink, hawks, owls, fox, and snakes.

One time I saw a dead mouse move. Using a broom I swept it out of the cabin, and while doing so noticed there was a large maggot feeding on the mouse. I later learned that the maggot was probably inside the mouse even when it was alive! The maggot came from a botfly, which lay their eggs near a mouse's burrow. The mouse ingests these eggs when grooming its fur. Then the eggs hatch inside the mouse and tiny maggots migrate to the mouse's groin. The maggots grow—some to an inch and a half long—creating a wound in the mouse's skin from which they can breathe, and when fully grown they pop out. That's why a mouse killed in a trap just seconds earlier can miraculously appear to move—a giant maggot is crawling around inside, still feeding off its host.

The old-fashioned mousetrap is probably the most effective means of ridding your home of mice. But how could I get rid of them in the weeks I was not at the cabin and unable to bait and empty the traps? Glue strips are out of the question, because the mouse dies a slow death—or even worse, is still alive when you check the trap. (The American Veterinary Medical Association recommends a "cervical dislocation," which means breaking their necks. I don't think so . . .) Poison works well, but you run the risk of mice crawling into walls to die and decay (and smell).

So I'm not too fond of mice in my cabin. That night after the storm, I was sleep deprived and stupid enough to think I could put a dent in their population by attacking them with a club. One of the critters ran into the cupboard, and I proceeded to whack away blindly, succeeding only in breaking five dishes. After this I finally rebaited all four traps and tried to sleep. On future trips I always set the traps immediately upon arrival, and by the second night of my stay I'd have a relatively quiet night.

It's not surprising that the cabin's guest book is filled with entries about mice. Some of the entries are from guests who never returned:

*Could not sleep. Decided to write a book on things to do by yourself in the dark while listening to mice. Will probably have limited but loyal readers.*

*Maintained combat position throughout the night to fend off attacking mice. By dawn, the enemy forces were reduced by three.*

*Matthew promised me a romantic weekend for two at Mike's cabin. Never in my wildest dreams did I expect to ward off rodents all night.*

CHAPTER 6

# TIME ON MY SIDE: BUILDING A NEW DEFINITION OF HOME IMPROVEMENT

*Shall we forever resign the joys of construction*
*to the carpenter?*
—HENRY DAVID THOREAU

On my next visit that summer, I took a good look around the inside of the cabin before going to bed and realized how strange this place must look to a first-time guest. The cabin was one big room. The ceiling was just under seven feet high and was uneven in spots. The walls were prefabricated tan paneling that Boomer, Cogs, and I had put up, and they too showed the evidence of amateur work. A large bureau separated the cabin into two sections. By the entry door was a fridge, cabinets, and a sink with no running water. In the back section I'd put an old couch, a double bed next to that, and two mattresses stacked against the far wall. That was it, except for the pull-down stairs that led to the second floor. Nobody ever bothered to go up there—too dark and musty.

*Boomer might be right,* I thought, *maybe I should start putting some money into the place and really fix it up.* But where would I start? The cabin had been built seven years ago by a farmer who wanted a little retreat, and he'd used secondhand materials. To fix it up I would basically have to tear it down and start over. And any improvements I made would hardly increase its value. Plus, I had no plans to sell the place—it meant too much to me.

What about adding water and indoor plumbing? That suggestion came up time and time again. Maybe I resisted out of stubbornness. Maybe someday. But the outhouse didn't bother me, and I could bring up all the water I needed in a ten-gallon container with a spigot. I rest the container by the side of the sink, and it's just like having a regular water faucet. For showers, I have a solar-heated Sun Shower: a three-ply black plastic bag that holds three gallons of water with a handheld showerhead "with flow control." The Sun Shower claims to rise to a toasty 107 degrees if left in the sun for three hours in 70-degree temperatures. Of course, the sun has a hard time reaching the little clearing by the cabin because of the towering canopy of trees above. The only time full sunshine penetrates the opening in the canopy is between November and April, when the trees, stripped bare of their leaves, aren't able to filter the sunlight.

At least I could improve upon the shower; the same company also made a Sun Shower enclosure. This is a plastic, tubelike stall that can be hung from a tree. All you need to do is step inside for complete privacy while showering in the woods. But no one is ever around on the mountain, so I held off on purchasing the one improvement I could afford. Besides, hardly anyone uses the Sun Shower in the first place; it's easier to dive in the pond.

I might have been afraid of bears, owls, porcupines, and a handful of other visitors, but I knew I wasn't afraid of roughing it. The way I saw it, if I "improved" the cabin, two things would happen. The first is that it would begin to feel like home, and one amenity would lead to another. Before you know it I'd have a satellite dish and spend my time lying on the couch watching sports. The improvements would disconnect me from the natural world, placing yet another layer between me and what was going on outside. Instead of getting away from civilization for a change of pace, I'd just be moving from one location to another without the experience of something entirely new. I *liked* the challenge of jumping in the pond on cool mornings. I liked cooking outside over an open fire. I liked that the cabin *didn't* have a TV, phone, or microwave. It was a pleasure to do some serious reading rather than watching TV, walking rather than driving, and going for a couple of days without seeing another soul or saying a word.

The other thing that would happen is that if I sank a bunch of money into the place, I'd feel obligated to come up every free weekend. I'd also start to worry about lightning, vandals, and whatnot. With the cabin in such a primitive state, I was worry free when I wasn't there. I didn't have to fret about pipes leaking or go through the chore of draining them at the end of the season. All I had to do was shut the door when I left.

Another suggestion made by friends who visited was that I should post the land. The first year, I did put up a "Keep Out" sign, but it bothered me every time I passed it. I was just starting to get over the mistaken notion that I owned the land and was coming to view my role as a steward. Sure, I didn't want somebody coming to the hill and cutting the trees down, but I didn't mind folks walking through. Nor did I mind hunters using the hill. I don't hunt, but I knew it was a way of life in rural areas, and the last thing I want to be is a flatlander keeping out the locals whose families had probably hunted these mountains for generations. So I took the "Keep Out" sign down.

I didn't even mind when I found that a hunter had built a blind on my land without asking my permission. The blind was so well hidden it had probably been there for a couple of years before I stumbled upon it. The two empty beer cans thrown on the ground annoyed me, but the blind itself was made out of wood and would soon settle back into the ground from which it came.

These were the thoughts that went through my mind as I settled down for the night. I wanted to try sleeping on the porch, but the mosquitoes would probably keep me awake. Then it hit me; I wanted a screened porch and small deck overlooking the cliff and pond. The porch would be the one improvement that would bring me closer to the outdoors. I would fall asleep to the sounds of whippoorwills, tree frogs, and owls, and awake to the chickadees, thrushes, and woodpeckers.

Instead of going to bed, I started working on a book idea I had been researching. If I could get it published, the proceeds would enable me to hire a contractor to expand the porch and add a deck. A wonderful plan: The experiences I had while at the cabin would enhance my writing, and my writing would in turn enhance the cabin.

I must have worked until midnight, when the cry of coyote roused me from the task at hand.

The other improvement I would make was to build a trail from the cabin down to the pond. One morning that same year, I woke with a plan to start on the trail, but while I brushed my teeth, I realized it had been three days since I had shaved or said a single word out loud.

I drove down to the café, not so much for the breakfast, but to talk to someone (other than the mice), even if it was just placing my order. I read the news while sipping coffee and was surprised by the headlines. A government had been overthrown, the stock market had tanked, and the annual flooding in Calcutta and famine in Central Africa continued unabated. When thinking about the socioeconomic struggles of the world compared to those in the natural world, I feel both are equally harsh, but at least I was learning to better understand the struggles of the natural world.

Instead of returning straight to the cabin, I went fishing on the Lamoille River. When I'm fishing I'm able to lose myself completely. I love to slowly and stealthily wade up the river, focusing completely on the current, casting without the trout seeing me or feeling the vibrations caused by my footsteps. I wade carefully and quietly, making long casts—hopefully before the fish are aware of my presence. When absorbed in such a pursuit, it's hard for any other thought to enter my mind. If I'm really lucky, just for a fleeting second I become part of the river, curling around the next bend, coursing through the rapids, alive, connected.

I fished for three straight hours, catching one tiny trout, but loving every minute of being in such a breathtaking setting. The river slow and serene in one stretch, then dashing and singing over boulders in another, enclosed by dark green hills on one side and pastureland on the other. A muskrat crossed the river ahead, a great blue heron took wing, and a dozen cows stared blankly as I made my way upstream.

When completely exhausted I returned to the car, driving a back road to a local swimming hole, where I walked a winding trail through hemlocks to a deep pool at the edge of a small waterfall. I laid a towel out, changed into my bathing suit, and eased my way into the icy water, loving the thrill of discovering yet another wonderful place so close to the cabin.

The waterfall cascades over a twenty-foot wall of granite, and I toyed with the idea of jumping from the top. I'd take a look. Making my way up the rocks heading toward the lip of the falls, my eyes widened when I reached the summit of the rock ledge. There lay two young women sunning themselves, totally naked.

I tried to act nonchalant, fighting the urge to stare. I offered a simple "hello." They made no move to cover themselves and probably assumed I had climbed up to jump off the cliff into the pool below. It was obvious they had laid claim to the sunny ledge.

What was the proper etiquette to assume when confronted by two nude young women? Taking my own bathing suit off was hardly the answer. I had already tried the friendly approach with no success. So instead I studied the edge of the ledge and peered down into the pool below. From up here it seemed much higher than twenty feet. I stole a glance back at the girls. They had rolled onto their stomachs and were watching me. Having their nakedness so near was making me uncomfortable, and I was the one left feeling awkward and exposed. I gave a stupid smile then hurled myself off the ledge.

I landed all wrong and many parts of my body hurt all at once. Later, I read a national travel magazine with instructions on how to make an emergency jump into a river from a height of more than twenty feet. Of the eight key points, I followed only the first two correctly: be sure the depth of the water is adequate, and jump feetfirst. Here are the others I failed to follow:

- Keep your body completely vertical. If your body is not straight, you can break your back upon entry.
- Squeeze your feet together.
- As you enter the water, clench your buttocks to prevent water from rushing in and causing severe internal damage.
- Protect your crotch by covering it with your hands.
- Immediately after you hit the water, spread your arms and legs wide and move them back and forth to generate resistance, which will slow your plunge.
- Swim to shore immediately after surfacing.

I've swum at those falls many times since, and left the high diving to the more daring.

When I returned to the cabin, I had recovered but walked a little funny. I attacked my chores with the vigor of a man who knows he escaped a close call that could have ended far worse than merely a few sore spots. First I picked up fallen branches from the driveway, then I cleaned the outhouse (digging out the pit where the porcupines used to live), and finally I built a bookcase.

I'm not Mr. Fix-it, but I enjoy making things, even if they turn out less than perfect. It's the idea of constructing something from scratch that is appealing. If I had the talent and the time, I would build my own cabin, as Thoreau did. Thoreau loved the process, writing in *Walden*: "Shall we forever resign the joys of construction to the carpenter?" In fact much of Thoreau's values and his lifestyle appeal to me. But there's a lot about Thoreau that is not as well known. For one, he lived with his parents for almost his entire life. And although he extolled the virtues of solitude at Walden Pond, he made frequent visits into town, often dropping in at his parents' home for dinner. Lastly, he made mistakes. No, he didn't make a hasty jump from a waterfall, tremble from the scream of a porcupine, or kill a harmless snake. He accidentally burnt down several forested acres of his beloved Concord woods. Thoreau was a brilliant thinker, but he was as human as the rest of us. He made me feel better about my learning curve.

When I finished the bookcase, I ate a late lunch and then began the type of project I like the best—trail making. The sheer physical labor, the sweat, the sense of accomplishment, and then knowing that a dip in the pond awaits makes this task a joy. Using branch clippers and a saw, I began at the cabin with the idea of fashioning a trail down a more gradual side of the hill to connect with an old logging road, then switchback for the final fifty yards to the edge of the pond, where I'd built a small dock. Rather than making a direct line to the pond, the switchback allowed for a more gradual descent and would minimize any erosion problems. I didn't have to take down any large trees, and mostly I used the clippers to remove low-lying branches. Working so close to the land, I noticed things I normally would have overlooked: a large piece of slate that I could use for the back of the outdoor fireplace, a huge quartz boulder that would make a nice trail seat, a branch with a burl (an odd bulbous growth) on it that could be fashioned into a war club.

Thinking about making the war club made me realize that as much as I've searched in my years wandering Vermont, I have never found any artifacts, even though the Abenaki once roamed the land. They generally lived in the fertile valleys and along the riverways or Lake Champlain, using the mountains for hunting.

But the concentration of Native Americans living in Vermont was small in comparison to the population of Nipmucks, Wampanoags, Narragansetts, Pequots, Mohegans, and other tribes that lived in southern New England.

The more I study Native Americans and their incredible knowledge of the natural world, the more I understand how interconnected their lives were with the earth itself. This relationship, born out of their spiritual beliefs, is also born out of survival. And the natives had centuries to perfect their art of surviving in the natural world. The first humans to enter New England were the Paleo-Indians, who arrived roughly twelve thousand years ago when the glaciers started to retreat. Vermont looked like the Arctic tundra, with a scattering of spruce and birch. Wooly mammoth, mastodon, and caribou roamed the land alongside beavers the size of black bears and rivers teeming with fish. The Paleo-Indians followed the movement of the herds, and these nomadic hunters used atlatls, or throwing sticks, to hurl their spears. The projectile points had grooves in each side where they were attached to the spear, and these fluted points have been found at sites in Vermont, such as Fairfax and Derby.

As I cleared the trail and cut the future war club, I couldn't help but think that for the last four days I had lived a little like the natives who lived here before me. Granted, I went to the village café rather than catching my own food, and I admit that both mice and bears had unnerved me, but I spent a few days without TV, phone, or computer. For some of us that's a big deal, akin to bringing down a woolly mammoth.

Also important was the fact that I was indulging myself by taking vacations, recognizing that time, not money, is our most important asset. People at my office routinely "lose" their vacation days because rules allow employees to carry over into the next year only a small number of vacation days—use it or lose it. A slick policy, especially when workers are afraid to take all their vacation, since they are pressured to produce more and more and a vacation will put them further behind. But buying the cabin prevented me from falling into that trap; I just had to be here as often as possible. The cabin was something to look forward to, something good for the soul. There was no way I was going to "lose" vacation days, because the only sure thing we really have at this very moment is time.

Entries in the guest book allude to the therapeutic powers of time away from the office and confirm what a wonderful world this can be. We don't know the pace we run until we stop.

*Enjoyed a late morning snooze to the sound of wrens. A day of such peace and beauty I will never forget.*

*Couldn't believe I actually sat still and watched a rainstorm sweep across the pond. Wonderful show.*

*Life is teeming everywhere, so many birds. I love the way the light falls on the ferns. I could stay forever.*

*Great to be at Toug's cabin. Time passes, our lives go in different directions, but here things never change. We act like kids again.*

# CHAPTER 7

# AN AVID READER LEARNS THE LESSONS OF THE FRONTIER

*These bear being so hard to die reather intimedates us all;*
*I must confess that I do not like the gentlemen*
*and had reather fight two Indians than one bear.*
—MERIWETHER LEWIS

Vermont's trout rivers, such as the Battenkill and the White Rivers, are legendary for fishing fanatics looking for trophy-size browns and rainbows. More than once I spent day trips driving south to those rivers as well as northeast to the Clyde and Connecticut and northwest to the Missisquoi and Lamoille. The small streams near the cabin, however, provided me with more satisfying outings, even though the trout were much smaller. What the streams lacked for in size of trout and volume of water they made up for in secluded setting, winding slowly through bright pastures then curling into forests of spruce and fir so dense that parts of the stream were probably never touched by the sun. Most were no more than three or four feet wide, with long stretches of shallow water from three inches to a foot in depth. But if I followed a stream long enough, I'd often be rewarded by a few deep pockets of water, usually located under the root system of a fallen tree or behind a large boulder. That's where the brook trout lived.

The streams demand complete attention when angling; one false step, one inadvertent shadow and the trout know you're there, and nothing will lure them from their lair. Carefully walking alongside a small stream and studying the water makes me feel more like a mink or an otter than a man, and I feel the tug of the wild within. Although there might be a few experts who could work a fly rod in such restricted conditions, my skill level certainly wasn't up to it, but I nevertheless challenged myself by using an ultralight spinning rod and a tiny lure rather than a hook and worm. Even in the pastures, casting was difficult because alders lined the stream bank, often creating an impenetrable tangle over the stream. The going was even tougher in the woods because of fallen logs; more than once I'd hook a fish only to have it shake free or break off when I couldn't get it out of a blowdown or over a log.

I would be completely focused before making a cast, lost in the moment, knowing the lure would have to land with pinpoint accuracy if I had any hope of fooling a trout. Sometimes the trout would be spooked; other times I'd see one follow the lure about five inches back, sensing something wasn't quite right. But the few times a strike came, it felt like receiving an electric jolt; it seems I'm always surprised at how hard a brookie can hit. And because the stream is small, the trout strikes no more than a few feet from where I'm standing, adding to the excitement.

Sometimes I never see a trout, but because I've been walking so quietly and am far from any road—probably fishing a stream that most anglers pass up—I see more wildlife when fishing these streams than at any other time. Once a raccoon came downstream while I was going upstream, and upon seeing each other we stopped and stared, connecting for just a second before the raccoon scampered off. Another time a deer was walking right up the middle of the stream, never seeing me crouched up on the bank. When it was ten feet away it caught my scent, pulling up abruptly, then wheeled around before dashing down the middle of the stream. Just as suddenly it stopped and looked back, as if doubting I was really a threat. My most memorable encounter occurred when I rounded a bend and heard a splash by a boulder in the middle of the stream up ahead. I froze and watched in amazement as three otters came out of the stream, climbed on the rock, and then wrestled as if playing king of the mountain, trying to knock one of the others off.

Catching the wild brook trout and seeing the raccoon, deer, and otter were all highlights of my cabin trips. Still, I couldn't help daydreaming about how much bigger the brook trout were and the variety and abundance of wildlife that had existed here before Europeans became established in America. Reading about the mountain men, the fur trappers, and explorers gave me a sense of what it would have been like to have lived in that time and inspired me to get closer to the land. Meriwether Lewis and William Clark in particular provided an unending source of knowledge and entertainment, while also fueling my imagination about bears.

Lewis had kept a detailed journal and wrote of a bear incident that he and his men caused when they spotted a grizzly bear on the riverbank while canoeing. Rather than ignore the bear, they paddled by, beached the canoes, and then circled back to surprise the bear. When they were within forty yards, four men discharged their rifles and all four balls hit the bear, two through the grizzly's lungs. However, the bear did not die; instead it rose up and charged. The men ran, and the bear chased them back to the canoes. Two of them paddled away and the others hid in the willows, where they fired at the bear, hitting it again. Once more the bear charged, and the men threw down their rifles and jumped into the river, with the bear close behind. It gained on one of the swimmers and was about to exact its revenge when one of the men who stayed on shore was able to shoot the bear through the head, killing it. When they examined the body, it was determined that eight balls had passed through its body.

Another time it was a bear that instigated the attack, choosing Lewis as its prey. When Lewis spotted the grizzly sneaking up on him, he took aim and squeezed the trigger. For a second, nothing happened; the rifle wasn't loaded. In Lewis's journal he describes how the bear charged "open-mouthed and full speed. I ran 80 yards and found he gained on me fast." Fortunately, Lewis ran right into the Medicine River, where he turned toward the bear "and presented the point of my espontoon." Lewis's courage saved him—the bear retreated. On my journey to becoming an outdoorsman, I wondered what I would have done in the same situation. Probably run to the water as Lewis had, but lacking the courage to turn and face the bear, I'd dive beneath the surface. The bear would have caught me like a salmon.

Despite his fortitude, Lewis does give us a glimpse of his fear and respect for the grizzlies when he writes "these bear being so hard to die reather intimedates us all; I must confess that I do not like the gentlemen and had reather fight two Indians than one bear."

Perhaps the most daring mountain man of all time was John Colter, a participant on the Lewis and Clark expedition. He met all the criteria Lewis outlined for the selection process of recruits: "good hunters, stout, healthy, unmarried men, accustomed to the woods and capable of bearing bodily fatigue in a pretty considerable degree." Colter was known for his marksmanship and soon became one of the chief hunters on the expedition. Sergeant John Ordway recorded how Colter became temporarily lost from the main group, but when found he had a rack of drying meat with more game than he could possibly eat. When another man was lost on the expedition, he was found half starved, having used all his lead bullets but killing only one rabbit.

Seeing the wilds of the west affected Colter more strongly than the other men of the expedition. While the party was returning to Saint Louis, he asked permission to return to the mountains with two trappers who had recently started for the northwest. Clark wrote that Colter had performed his duty so well "we agreed to allow him the privilage" of leaving the party, so long as no other men wanted to separate. It seems the other men couldn't wait to return to civilization, and Colter was the only member to stay in the wilds.

Long before I read about Colter and Lewis and Clark, I was searching out books about adventure in remote places. Each summer in high school I would scour the library, uncovering such gems as *North to Cree Lake,* by Art Karras, and *Two Against the North,* by Farley Mowat. I also found a few stories about lesser-known explorers such as John Ledyard, who sailed the seas with Captain Cook and trekked halfway across Siberia. Closer to home he built a dugout canoe at Dartmouth College and rode it down the Connecticut River to his home in Connecticut. Stories like that worked their way under my skin and subconsciously prompted me to later paddle most of the Connecticut River over a series of weekends, chronicling the trip in my 2001 book *River Days.* Another influence on my imagination was a book written by an unlikely author, TV correspondent Eric Sevareid, who penned a wonderful story of a daring journey he and a friend made to a remote region of Canada. Reading Sevareid's book, I felt that once he accomplished his journey, no other obstacle seemed too tough to tackle. What I learned from all my reading was one basic lesson: An education from nature can help you to appreciate life. It can prepare you for life by fostering ingenuity and resourcefulness. You learn quickly that to succeed over tough endeavors often depends on your adaptability and flexibility.

Reading about real mountain men was always humbling and inspiring. Those men were tougher than I will ever be. Still, their stories kept me reading late into the night, imagining the fascinating places where game was bountiful, rivers ran free, and there was not a sign of humankind for miles.

I think I've been chasing that dreamlike landscape all my life, hoping to find a remnant of the wilderness. Some people might argue that wilderness no longer exists in America, but I found a wild pocket of land around the cabin. Rather than just focusing on improving my woods skills, I began to think in terms of what the future might hold for the hills around the cabin and what I could do to protect the beauty of the place. I wanted to take it a step beyond the mountain-man adventures.

The first thing I promised myself is that I would never have the land logged just to make a few bucks. As it is, we have almost no significant tracks of old-growth forest in New England, because at one time or another most of our woods were cut at least once for lumber or to make pastureland for sheep and cattle. Although I didn't know it at the time, I was slowly coming to the realization that I could be a steward to my six acres rather than "taming" it. I decided to not introduce any new plants, shrubs, or trees but to leave the protective vegetation near the pond just as it is. How could I improve upon the Blue Flag irises that flower violet-blue along the pond each summer? My driveway would remain as a dirt lane rather than paved, and the tiny patch of grass in the clearing would stay tiny, with no "lawn care." The last thing I wanted to have happen was to have fertilizers and pesticides from a lawn leaching into the pond.

In some respects second home owners are like the mountain men themselves, subduing the very thing they love the most and introducing irrevocable change, such as killing grizzlies, beavers, and buffalo. Writer A. B. Gutherie Jr., perhaps the quintessential writer on mountain men, recognized this very contradiction. In his novel *The Big Sky,* there is a scene where two mountain men suddenly realize this fact: "We went to get away and to enj'y ourselves free and easy, but folks was bound to foller and beaver to get scarce and Injuns to be killed or tamed, and all the time the country gettin' safer and better known. We ain't seen the end of it yet, Boone, not to what the mountain man does against hisself. Next thing is to hire out for guides and take parties acrost and sp'ile the county more."

Yes, the mountain men influenced me, but by now I realized the land around me didn't need conquering, just protecting.

Although most of the original forest of New England has been cut, huge tracks of land still have little or no development. The reason is simple—they are owned by the paper companies. I once had a bird's-eye view of just how expansive these forests are when

I went up in a floatplane in northern Maine for a trip that combined fishing, canoeing, and research for a piece I was writing.

It was quite a shock flying from the mayhem of Logan Airport in Boston to the tiny airport in Presque Isle, Maine. (To give you an idea of just how small the Presque Isle Airport is, consider that when you're flying out of there, the same man who issues you a boarding pass later appears out on the runway with signal wands, directing your plane to its takeoff position.) From the Presque Isle Airport a shuttle car took me to a nearby lake where the floatplane waited. The four-seat Cessna taxied to the end of the lake, then roared to life at full throttle, skimming across the water before becoming airborne.

Just five minutes out of Presque Isle, the signs of civilization ended, save for an occasional logging road twisting through seemingly endless miles of forest. While the forest stretched out in all directions I could easily see it was being worked, spotting where logging crews had clear-cut, strip-cut and selectively cut. Most people are concerned about the clear-cut technique because the land is stripped of every single tree. Another concern is what happens after the land is cleared. To prevent opportunistic plants such as raspberries and trees such as popple, or poplar, and pin cherry from shading the slower-growing conifers, herbicides are sprayed on the land. The deciduous plants and trees are killed, and the forest is allowed to come back as a monoculture profit center of the most valuable lumber, spruce and fir.

Looking down from the floatplane, I remembered a book I had read—*Hatchet,* by Gary Paulson. I kind of wish I had never read it. The story begins with a young boy flying in a floatplane to visit his dad, who's working in the wilds of Canada. Like me, the boy loves flying in the little plane, amazed at the expanse of forest below. The only problem with flying one of these little planes is there is no copilot. If something happens to the pilot, you're on your own. Well, in the book something happens to the pilot. He is stricken by a heart attack, and the boy struggles to fly the floatplane, eventually making a crash landing in a lake. I remember looking closely at my pilot after thinking of *Hatchet,* examining him for signs of stress, guessing how overweight he might be, and taking note of what he was doing with the steering wheel. Just in case.

That got me to asking him some very normal flying questions. "You ever crash?"

He looked at me kind of funny. "The real question you should be asking is if I've crashed more than once."

"Why?"

"Because once is OK, maybe a good thing, because the pilot learns from it. But if it happens again, I'd wonder."

"So have you crashed?"

"Once," he said.

"What happened?"

"It was an old plane, with fabric wings. The fabric tore, and I was in a semidive, not really able to steer the plane. I was preparing for what they call a treetop landing. Just then a field came into view and I was able to squash her down. I'll tell you, after that I believe in God."

I looked below. There were no fields, nor were there any lakes to be seen. If something happened, it would be a treetop landing. Like I said, I wished I had never read *Hatchet*.

We only flew at a thousand feet, and I was able to see a couple of moose down below feeding in a bog. If a person wanted to be a mountain man in the lower forty-eight, this would be as good a location as any. Two people who did just that—at least for a short period of time—were Henry Thoreau in the mid-1800s and Joe Knowles in the early-1900s. Their stories are quite different, but both fascinated me—Thoreau's because he was humbled by his experience, and Knowles's because of the mystery surrounding his adventure.

Thoreau first visited the Maine North Woods in 1846, making an arduous paddling and hiking trip that taught him a lesson about just how wild this country could be. (He also realized that his woods skills left something to be desired, when a spark from his campfire burned his tent to the ground. He spent the night sleeping under his boat, with his feet sticking out toward the campfire.) Thoreau climbed Mount Katahdin and discovered it to be a far different place than the friendly confines of Walden Pond, finding this side of nature to be fearsome and vast, an "inhuman Nature." This raw, unforgiving side of nature was new to Thoreau, giving him a scare but nevertheless providing a new source of fascination, and he returned to the Maine Woods several times thereafter.

While Thoreau's experiences in the Maine Woods are still celebrated today, Joe Knowles's exploits have largely been forgotten. Knowles, a part-time artist, claimed he could walk into the Maine Woods totally naked and survive for sixty days. The media loved the idea, and in August of 1913 reporters followed Knowles to the shores of King and Bartlett Lakes in western Maine, watching him walk into the wilds with nothing more than a loincloth. What happened over the next sixty days will never be known for sure. Knowles did survive, and people hailed him as a hero. How he survived is still open to debate.

Knowles claimed he followed a game trail to Lost Pond and then, using a club, killed a black bear, saying he skinned it with a piece of slate and used its hide for a blanket and clothing. When reporters later doubted the story, Knowles insisted on showing them exactly how he did it, and some unfortunate bear was brought to Knowles, who sure enough brained it with a club. One thing he couldn't explain was a cabin on the shores of Lost Pond. Knowles said he never saw it, but a new version of his weeks in the woods began to emerge that had him staying at the cabin with a reporter friend, enjoying beans and campfires, while the two of them brainstormed a book that would chronicle his adventure and make them both rich. Another version of the story came from two guides who claimed they were in cahoots with Knowles and left some clothes, food, and even beer for him in the woods.

If Knowles was telling the truth and he really did survive for sixty days in the woods, that was quite a feat. I think I had a little of Knowles in me, wanting to prove to myself I could survive in the woods, but too chicken to actually go into the forest and try. John Colter I wasn't, but I did test the waters in a small way while at the cabin, trying to live off the land for a three-day period in May of my third year of owning the cabin.

I didn't set any elaborate rules, but I did wear something more than a loincloth (imagine my neighbors if I went by on the pink bike wearing nothing but a loincloth), and decided not to use any traps or nets, although a fishing rod was allowed. The easy part was catching a few trout, but they hardly provided sustenance and certainly didn't put a dent in my hunger. I even tried eating a pickerel, but spent more time picking bones out of my mouth than swallowing fish. Aside from the fish, I foraged in the woods and thought I hit the jackpot when I picked a bucket of fiddle-head ferns. I boiled them, cheated a little by adding butter, then dug in and promptly gagged. They were incredibly bitter and dry, and tasted as if someone had just stuffed a pair of Boomer's socks in my mouth. I later learned that my mistake was picking them too late in the season; the plants I picked were about a foot tall and the fiddle shape was becoming unfurled. Proper collection should occur when the plants are less than six inches tall and the fronds are still tightly curled.

I thought foraging might also yield berries, but there's only a brief window from mid-July to mid-August when blueberries and raspberries are ripe, and my timing was wrong. So on day one of my experiment I went to bed hungry, rereading Euell Gibbons's *Stalking the Wild Asparagus.* Gibbons's book was not limited to eating plants, but included animals too, such as Woodchuck in Sour Cream and Basted Muskrat. If those were not to my liking, there was always Raccoon Pie: "To make Raccoon Pie," Gibbons writes, "disjoint a young 'coon and soak the pieces in a salt-vine-gar solution . . ." Hmmm, I was hungry but not *that* hungry. Gibbons seemed to chide me with his closing lines in the chapter on the meat course: "An ingenious forager who is also a clever cook need never go without some tasty wild meat. There is always good hunting and good eating for the true neoprimitive who has a strong stomach and weak prejudices." I have neither when it comes to eating (and killing) a raccoon, possum, or muskrat. And so I turned my attention to his chapters on wild onions, grapes, artichokes, and anything else that did not crawl, walk, or run.

The next morning I was up early, hoping old Euell's tips would put breakfast on the table. I walked through three fields looking for wild asparagus, strawberries, and even dandelion leaves with-out success. Then I searched a marsh for cattails (to dig up the roots) and again came up empty-handed. Next I tried turning over rocks in a stream and actually caught two crayfish. Each was about two inches long, and I couldn't imagine there was enough meat to warrant expending the energy of boiling them, so I let them go.

By noon I was ravenous, acknowledged my failure, and drove to town, where I stuffed my face. The experience enlightened me to just how much food I eat in a day and how difficult foraging would be for long-term health, even if my training were better. I'm content now to go blueberry and raspberry picking on occasion, but I leave the crayfish to the raccoons and fiddleheads to the serious forager.

My guest book entry for that trip says it all . . .

*Tried to live off the land, with little luck. Found out that I'd have to eat about ten brook trout to stop the hunger for a while. Would a real mountain man have quit so easily and headed for the nearest diner?*

# CHAPTER 8

# ON GETTING LOST AND FINDING JOHN MUIR

*Thousands of tired, nerve-shaken, over-civilized people are beginning to find out that going to the mountains is going home: that wilderness is a necessity.*

—JOHN MUIR

By my fourth year at the cabin, I had conquered my fears of bears and snakes and had even learned to accept the wonder of nearby lightning and thunder with respect rather than terror. For a cream puff from the suburbs, I was starting to feel pretty heady. Until the day, just one mile from the A-frame, it happened.

I got lost.

I made a series of mistakes that day, probably due to my spring-time exuberance. My first mistake was not paying attention to my surroundings as I tramped through the woods trying to find a hidden trout pond I'd heard about. The trees hadn't leafed out yet, so I thought the visibility would make it easy to retrace my steps.

I started out at about noon, bushwhacking in a generally uphill direction, making slow but steady headway, climbing over a series of blowdowns and through a swampy area. There was no pond in sight, not even a stream, and after about a half hour I decided to head back. It took me just five minutes of walking to realize something was wrong. I should have hit the swamp, but instead I was on high ground. I tried altering my course a little, but still no swamp—just dense, dark stands of maple, fir, and spruce. Using a large boulder as my "home base," I set out in a circle, trying to find the wetland that should have been within a stone's throw. Nothing looked familiar, and I went back to the boulder fully aware I was perspiring from walking way too fast.

A sense of unease was rising in me with each step, and I tried to force it down to the pit of my stomach. The fear felt like a flame that jumps from a fire pit and finds tinder-dry wood to feed on, expanding by the second. In my case the flame of fear was feeding on my uncertainties. I couldn't remember the last time I had such a feeling of dread, and I knew I couldn't let the fear turn into a full-blown panic.

At the boulder I wanted to push off in a new direction, but I got hold of my emotions and forced myself to stop for a minute and take stock of my situation. My first thought: *Nobody knows where I am.* Even if I had left a note at the cabin (which I should have done), it would be days before my roommates down in Boston would begin to worry. I did have my daypack, with water—thank God—camera, toilet paper, deer call, bug dope, and compass. I got the compass out. Now I could locate north, but still did not know where I was standing. When I started out, I thought I'd been walking in a straight line from my car, but I hadn't bothered to use the compass, so I could have walked in a circle for all I knew. (I later learned it's almost impossible to walk in a straight line for an extended period of time in the woods without a compass.)

It was becoming clear that I really didn't know how to use the compass I'd been carrying in my pack for the last few years. It was next to useless because I hadn't noted which direction my car was before I started walking. A topographical map would have helped, but instead I had packed a deer call. Great, I'd blow on the call, and help in the form of a lonesome buck would be on the way. The other item I should have had in the pack was water-proof matches. I instinctively knew that if I had to spend the night in the woods, a fire would have given me the psychological boost to make it bearable.

So I sat there and went over what few options I did have, courtesy of reading so many mountain-man books: Option one: *Use the sun to tell direction.* It was overcast. Option two: *Use the North Star to tell direction.* Not a good choice; it was still daylight and I didn't want to be there in the dark, nor did I think walking at night would be safe. Option three: *Follow a stream until it leads to a bigger stream, which will eventually spill into a river, where there will likely be a town.* I had not passed a stream, and even if I did, it might lead me away from my car and take forever to merge with a river. Option four: *Scream like bloody hell*—no, that would make the panic rise; just think of the chill it would give you to hear your own howl echoing back through the forest.

After going through my options, the smartest thing I did was to stay sitting and not follow the temptation to push on. This was the one time all of my mountain-man reading was coming in handy—I'd read plenty of horror stories of men crashing wildly though the woods to escape the terror of being alone. And "alone" is the operative word when it comes to the fear that was building inside of me.

This may sound odd to those who have never faced such dread, but no less an authority than mountaineer Joe Simpson, author of *Dark Shadows Falling,* confirms that all of us dread the thought of checking out totally alone. Simpson had fallen into a crevasse in the Peruvian Mountains and had broken his leg, writing, "Only the overwhelming desire not to die alone, slowly and without human company, kept me going." He began crawling, and in four-and-a-half days (losing nearly 40 percent of his body weight to dehydration and exertion) he made it to base camp.

Joe Simpson faced death. At the most, I probably faced a cold, lonely night in the woods, but that didn't make it any less terrifying for a neophyte.

I knew I was wasting time just sitting on the rock considering my options, and the late hour of the afternoon was not lost on me, especially with the temperature already down to the forties. Even though it was April, I still faced the risk of hypothermia if I spent the night there. Would I even know when I entered the danger zone of hypothermia? Slurred speech is one sure sign, but who would I talk to? Who would tell me I was slurring? Lack of coordination is another telltale sign, but would I notice? Probably the only warning I couldn't miss would be nonstop shivering. If I had to spend the night in the woods, I was going to use the half hour before darkness to prepare. First I would find a large fallen log, or maybe even use the boulder I was sitting on, to block the wind. Then I'd pile hemlock boughs below me to keep my body off the damp ground and pile more on top, along with dry leaves to act as insulation. If it rained I'd be in serious trouble, but maybe sheets of birch bark would help if I could locate a tree big enough.

These were the thoughts that ran through my mind. An active imagination certainly doesn't help, nor does all the reading about outdoor adventure. I'd recently read Jack London's *To Build a Fire,* and that only served to make me more nervous. In the story, which is set in the Yukon, the main character is out in subzero weather when he slips through the ice. He escapes the water but knows he must get a fire going immediately, which he does. Calamity strikes when the heat from the fire warms the snow on a tree limb above, dumping the snow directly onto the fire and extinguishing it. Unable to get the fire rekindled, and unable to find the coordination to strike a match, he grabs his dog, thinking he will kill the dog and be able to warm his hands inside the dog's body. He gets the dog in a bear hug, but his fingers are unable to grasp his knife or choke the dog. The cold does its work, and the man dies.

Much later I reread *To Build a Fire* and learned that London also thought imagination can be an asset in the woods. Imagination brings about a healthy dose of fear by having the mind jump ahead to worst-case scenarios, and fear can prevent a person from getting in trouble in the first place. Of the man in *To Build a Fire,* London wrote:

> The trouble with him was that he was without imagination. He was quick and alert in the things of life. But only in the things, and not in the significances. Fifty degrees below zero meant eighty-odd degrees of frost. Such fact impressed him as being cold and uncomfortable, and that was all. It did not lead him to meditate upon his frailty as a creature of temperature, and upon man's

frailty in general, able only to live within certain narrow limits of heat and cold; and from there on it did not lead him to the conjectural field of immortality and man's place in the universe.

I sat on that boulder for a good twenty minutes. I was not calm and composed, but rather so fearful of making the wrong decision I hesitated setting off again. I knew if I made the wrong choice I really would be spending the night in the woods. Finally I decided to just head to the southeast, which I guessed was in the opposite direction I had first set out from the car, thinking that would at least bring me back to the road. After just a couple hundred feet of walking, I found that I was going up an incline when I should have been going down. I fought the urge to turn back and in a short distance was relieved to see level ground again. I walked for a solid hour, much longer than my original walk from the car. Even though the temperature was about fifty degrees, I was sweating, and the thought of spending the night in a cold, clammy shirt made me feel like crying.

It was 5:00 and soon it would be dark. I stopped at a large log and told myself this is where I'd spend the night and that all would be fine. Then I heard the most wonderful sound in the world. A car engine. I was no more than forty feet from the road. I ran to the road and literally started skipping back to my car. The only problem was that I was so disoriented I went in the wrong direction. An hour later I flagged down a motorist and explained I wasn't sure which direction to go. He asked for details about where I'd parked, and after I told him he quickly said, "I know about where it is, and you're a good three miles away. I'll give you a lift."

Back at the cabin I drank cup after cup of hot chocolate, feeling quite grateful to be out of the woods and determined not to get lost again. I picked up pen and paper and wrote down what I would carry in my daypack in the future: matches in a waterproof container, water, maps, compass, whistle (for blowing if a search party is out), and a knife. I would also improve my map and compass skills. Then I thought of one other thing I simply could not do without—a second set of eyeglasses. (Once, while skinny-dipping in a mountain river, I came out of the water and located my clothing but could not find my glasses. I started walking out but could barely make out the trail, let alone the rocks and roots that were tripping me up. Back I went for one final search, and through a stroke of luck found my glasses on a rock about two feet away from where I'd left my clothes.)

I sat on the porch, toasty warm in a down jacket, and thought about how my pack would help me in a jam. I'd come to realize that the most important survival tool is right between your ears. Simply asking yourself "What's the safe course of action?" can make all the difference.

I now focus on "staying found." I usually stay on a trail or near a stream or river, and if I'm bushwhacking I try to study a topographical map first and take it with me. Now when I go off trail, I remember that April afternoon and it gives me a healthy dose of caution.

Not long after my experience of being lost, I began to read about John Muir, who quickly became my favorite mountain man. I also began to feel a little embarrassed about the terror I had felt over being lost for a few hours, when I learned that Muir, at age twenty-eight, walked a thousand miles, from Indianapolis to Florida, taking the "wildest, leafiest, and least trodden way." An excellent biography of Muir is *The Life and Adventures of John Muir* by James Clarke, who explained that when Muir took his thousand-mile walk, he did take map and compass but little else—just the clothes on his back, a plant press to keep specimens, a change of underwear, some toilet articles, and three books: the New Testament, John Milton's *Paradise Lost,* and the poetry of Robert Burns. I would need a support van to carry all the equipment I'd want to take.

Muir took this walk as a reaction to a terrible accident. He was working in a factory when a file pierced his right eye, causing the aqueous humor (the slippery material that protects the eye) to dribble out into his palm. He quickly lost his vision in that eye and later, perhaps from the shock, lost his vision in the other eye. How devastated he must have been, thinking he would never again see mountains, rivers, flowers, and the wild creatures. In time, however, he recovered, and when he did he made a life-altering decision. He quit his job at the factory, telling friends and family he was walking to the Gulf of Mexico as the start of his new life of "studying God's inventions." His first entry in his journal was signed "John Muir, Earthplanet, Universe."

After arriving in Florida, followed by a brief visit to Cuba, Muir purchased a berth on a ship sailing to California. One visit to Yosemite Valley and Muir knew he had found his special place and himself. His elation over the beauty of the valley was to turn into his lifework of speaking out for the preservation of the wilderness. He went on to found the Sierra Club to protect and preserve the western mountains, modeling it after the Appalachian Mountain Club in the east.

Like Henry Thoreau and Ralph Waldo Emerson, Muir sensed that saving the forests was important not only to our environment, but also to our spiritual selves. "Thousands of tired, nerve-shaken, over-civilized people," he wrote, "are beginning to find out that going to the mountains is going home: that wilderness is a necessity. Everybody needs beauty as well as bread, places to play in and pray in, where Nature may heal and cheer and give strength to body and soul alike." He saw the value in wilderness as not just a special place, but as intrinsically important for health and instruction, often referring to his own life as one of education at the "University of the Wilderness."

When I read that phrase, something clicked in me about my own relationship to the cabin and my six acres. Yes, I thought, Muir had crystallized what I was groping about for: The cabin was my university. Muir also taught me that the secret to real learning is through stillness. Only when we are still can we truly observe.

I don't think Muir was ever lost for a minute in the forest, even though there were many times when he didn't know exactly where he was standing. Being lost implies that a person is trying to get out of the woods but cannot. Muir, on the other hand, was so comfortable in the wild he felt free to wander, often covering hundreds of miles in an outing with just his bread, tea, and blanket. He thought nothing of walking twenty-five miles a day. He slept on mountaintops, in hollows, and once on a rock in the middle of a stream, just to hear the water better.

Yes, of all my heroes, Muir is my favorite mountain man, because he was in the woods simply to be in the woods. He was not trapping, he was not carving out a new trail, he was not fighting bears; he went to the woods to learn and renew. In a letter to his friend Mrs. Carr, he wrote, "[H]ow glorious my studies seem and how simple. I was alone and during the whole excursion, or period rather, was in a kind of calm incurable ecstasy. I am hopelessly and forever a mountaineer."

A few times I had fleeting feelings similar to ecstasy in the woods, but what I really desired was to attain Muir's comfort level, and I counted on the "University of the Wilderness" to help show me the way.

My guest book entry for that spring weekend was decidedly short, and the only reference I made to getting lost was this line:

*It was a long winter away from the cabin, but the few hours I spent lost were longer. Getting lost is not an experience I ever want to repeat.*

# CHAPTER 9

# EXPECT THE UNEXPECTED

*How many hearts with warm red blood in them are beating under cover of the woods, and how many teeth and eyes are shining! A multitude of animal people, intimately related to us, but of whose lives we know almost nothing.*
—JOHN MUIR

While getting lost made me realize my vulnerability, the cabin still provided its own share of "character-building" experiences. In my fourth year of ownership, I often went to the cabin alone, arriving at dark filled with anticipation for the weekend. I had learned that if I came straight from work, driving the four hours listening to the radio, I should allow for a transition period to adjust to the stillness of the woods. Rather than go straight to bed, I would often read first or walk down to the pond with a flashlight and take a few casts for bass. In this way I'd kick back into my slower "woods mode" and get acclimated to the quiet.

In those early days I did not own a four-wheel-drive car, and I had to park at the base of my steep, rutted driveway and walk the remaining quarter mile to the cabin. It was a grueling, multitrip affair, carrying all manner of gear, including a ten-gallon container of water that weighed close to eighty pounds. I always had a flashlight with me, not only for nighttime climbs up the driveway, but also because the cabin would sometimes lose power for hours at a time, particularly if a storm passed through. When the cabin wasn't in use, I always switched off the circuit breakers, thinking that was the safest thing to do to avoid power surges and fire. So whenever I arrived at the cabin, it would be pitch black, and the first thing I would do is walk with a flashlight to the main trip switch at the back of the cabin.

Most arrivals were uneventful, but there was one memorable trip in my fifth summer when I went to the cabin at night alone. I finished bringing up the last pile of gear from my car, stowing it on the porch, and opened the cabin's locked door, shining my flashlight on the electrical box on the back wall. While I padded across the cabin, the light from the swinging flashlight briefly illuminated something dark in the corner by the bed. I shined the beam directly on it and froze, not believing my eyes. My heart did a little flip-flop and I staggered back, dropping the flashlight, which, naturally, went out.

In that moment I saw a bear, its mouth open in a snarl, crouching behind the bed.

Surrounded now by total darkness, I assumed the bear was still crouching in the corner because, except for the sound of the flashlight hitting the floor, it was dead silent. It flashed through my mind that this must be the same bear I had seen in the logging field. I didn't move a muscle, but I knew the bear could locate me simply from the pounding of my heart.

I waited an eternity—probably three seconds—before I slowly reached down for the flashlight. I wasn't stupid enough to turn it on, but instead brandished it like a weapon, figuring if the bear charged I could club it on the snout before I passed out with fright.

Slowly, I backed up—right into something solid—and spun around, flicking the flashlight on. When I realized it was the dining table I'd backed into, I swung the light back toward the bear, expecting it to be charging toward me.

The bear's head was in the exact same position as before, its mouth still open, showing its gleaming white teeth. Why didn't it attack or roar? Why didn't it move at all?

I summoned up my mountain-man nerve and moved a few steps closer.

Then I could see why it didn't move. The bear had no body. It was just a mounted bear's head, propped on a chair behind the bed.

I could have killed my brother. This was not funny. What if I had had a heart attack, or even worse, what if I had brought a girl up here? I might have pushed her toward the bear and then made a dash out the door. When I calmed down, I got my things from the porch and settled in.

Later, when I decided to spend the last day of that three-day weekend fishing the Lamoille River, I learned that the mounted bear's head was a harbinger of the real thing. I was working my way up a remote section of the river in a pair of hip waders when I came upon a stretch of water that looked deeper than the top of my waders. Leaving the water, I slowly made my way through four-foot-high ferns along the bank. Suddenly, about eight feet ahead, a deep guttural "woof" rang out. The brush shook and I got a glimpse of something black, which moved but did not leave. Immediately I backed up a couple of paces, knowing this was a real bear—both head *and* body—and not a practical joke. I was shaking, knowing that in another few steps I would have surprised the sleeping bear.

I backtracked to the water, keeping my eye on the exact spot where the bear was apparently holding ground. This was not like the bear Bob and I had seen on the logging field, which, upon getting a whiff of us took off with such force it seemed to knock down trees while fleeing. For some reason this bear stayed put.

As I walked to the water, my courage began to build. I was becoming more aware of my surroundings and less frightened of the woodland creatures. My days of running from porcupines, diving for cover from bats, and cowering from the mighty white-footed mouse were over. Here I had a chance to show some pluck. Instead of returning back down the stream to my car, I decided to give the bear room but continue upstream. I took off my waders, pants, and underwear, flung them over my shoulder, and entered the river, cautiously wading, keeping well away from the bear's side. I half expected it to let out another "woof" and come dashing down into the water.

I could just picture what the search teams would find when they came looking for me. They would scratch their heads wondering how the bear had eaten every single bit of my body but left my pants and underwear without so much as a claw mark. I could hear them explaining to my parents: "We're awful sorry, couldn't find a trace of him. The tracks showed a bear attack. Seems like an open-and-shut case of bad timing and bad luck. Still don't know how the bear got your son out of his pants. Was it his habit to fish in the nude? Well, no matter; here are the few things we found at the accident site. Nice pair of powder blue polyester pants."

The bear never moved from its concealed location, and I made my way around and up the river without incident. Later, while eating lunch along the river, I got a cold clammy chill, thinking that perhaps the reason the bear didn't run was that her cubs were nearby. That bothered me. Everyone knows that black bears rarely attack, *except* when with cubs or when cornered or surprised. I probably surprised the bear and it felt cornered and had to make a stand to protect its cubs. I can't be sure, but that could be the scenario, so I felt lucky.

Still, despite my jitters, I was thrilled, and in a way honored, to have had the experience of glimpsing my second bear. Many in the northeast go their whole lives without seeing a bear. Just knowing that something as big and as wild as a black bear still roams the woods gave me a satisfied feeling that humans have not yet ruined everything. In fact, because so much of New England's former farmland has reverted to forest, and because conservation groups work hard to protect open space in northern New England, the bear population is actually quite healthy. But as humans build homes in bear habitats, the number of encounters with bears has been growing.

Walking down rivers can lead to adventure, other than encounters with bears. That same summer, Boomer and I camped along the Lamoille River during two days of intermittent rain. The good fishing made up for the wet camping. I was feeling quite pleased, wading along the banks of the river in an old pair of sneakers, casting into the rapids, when a strange thing happened. One minute I was on a gravel bank and the next I was up to my waist in a sand, mud, and water mixture. It all happened so fast I only had time to throw my rod to the side and spread my arms.

When I think of quicksand, images of the old Tarzan movies come to mind. Usually some European hunter is enjoying his safari in Africa, when he unknowingly steps in quicksand and in the blink of an eye sinks like a rock. He struggles to keep his nose and mouth above the slop. The last image we see is that of his hand reaching out, which also soon disappears, leaving only his white safari hat on the surface of the quicksand.

That's not exactly what happened to me. In the broad sense, quicksand or any quagmire is just ordinary sand or dirt mixed with upwelling water that acts like liquid. (It's a rare phenomenon and is usually confined to locations along rivers and wetlands.) When you try to pull yourself out, you have to work against the vacuum left behind, and as you transfer weight to the leg still in the quagmire, you sink even deeper.

When I went in I dropped to thigh level, squirmed around, and was quickly up to my waist. I screamed for Boomer. No answer. I couldn't believe I was stuck. Never in all my years of fishing had I been in mud beyond my ankles, and this pit seemed bottomless. An alder tree grew only three feet away, and I leaned toward it, letting my stomach spread out on the surface. I caught hold of the branch and started to pull. I felt one sneaker pop off, and this seemed to free me just enough to continue making progress to the shore.

That's when Boomer showed up.

"What happened?"

That was about the worst thing he could have said to a panicked, claustrophobic person twisting ever deeper into a brown hole.

"Just get me out! It feels like something's pulling at me."

Boomer got down on his knees, so that his head was just a couple of feet away. "Wow, I've never seen quicksand up here; it's really got you good. This is totally amazing. You're lucky you weren't wearing your waders, you'd be halfway to China. I think . . ."

I cut him off. "Pull me out now, you jerk!"

He could have walked away, driven into town and had a leisurely breakfast, read the paper, and then come back to check on me. I know he was thinking that, because he hesitated before extending his arm. I wanted to pull him in with a sudden yank, but then we'd both be stuck. Boomer got me out, minus one sneaker. I thanked him, walked a few feet upstream, and jumped into the river to get the sand and mud off.

Later I read up on the best technique to get yourself out of quicksand. One publication said to carry a pole, and when you start to sink lay the pole on the surface, then flop on your back on top of the pole. Equilibrium will be achieved, you will no longer sink, and you can pull one leg out at a time. I also consulted my trusty copy of *How to Stay Alive in the Woods,* in which Bradford Angier says, "[W]hen you get very far into the mire your body will probably be lighter than the semisolid it displaces, and you will stop sinking." Then as if directed at me, he wrote, "You will not go deeper, that is, unless you worm and twist your way down, trying ineffectually to get away. The thing to do therefore, is to present as much body area to the surface of the mire as may be necessary, and to do this with the utmost promptness."

Despite my close call in the mud on the Lamoille, I had learned a few things about the natural world, particularly when it came to identifying trees. The realization that I had increased my knowledge of the woods hit me when Boomer—of all people—paid me a compliment when I helped him distinguish various species of evergreens.

"I can never tell all these conifers apart," remarked Boomer as we drove from the river toward Hardwick. "They all look the same until you're up close."

"Yeah," I answered, "the toughest two are the red spruce and balsam fir. Both are about the same color, and from a distance their branches look alike. But here's a little trick. Try looking at their tops. The crown of the fir is tight and pointed like a spire, while the spruce is not nearly so neat and has a rounded top."

Boomer stared out the window. "That's pretty good." He paused, then added, "All this time you've been spending alone in the woods has some benefits after all. Trivia to be sure, but very impressive."

"And for lesson number two," I said proudly, "note how the hemlock has a shaggy look. And then there's the white pine, on which from a distance you can usually distinguish individual branches. The pine's foliage is clumped toward the end of the twigs. And of course let us not forget the noble tamarack, which is best described as a deciduous conifer. It's got kind of a wispy look and actually loses its needles in the fall. At the pond there is a nice stand of tamaracks opposite our dock. When we're there, I might paddle you over for some field study."

Boomer nodded like a teenager who suddenly realizes his parent isn't as stupid as he thought. "You've come a long way since the fourth grade."

Oh, I was feeling pretty good about myself. I even had a smug little grin I was trying to hide from Boomer. Didn't want to hurt the lad's feelings.

To capitalize on my show of knowledge, I actually pulled the car over to the road's shoulder (against Boomer's protest of "enough") to show him a stand of yellow birch—"not to be confused with white birch," I added. This proved to be my downfall, because as we got out of the car a bird landed on a branch in front of us.

"And what kind of bird is that?" asked Boomer.

I hesitated and looked the bird up and down. "That's called a little-gray-and-white-bird-with-a-short-neck. Don't recall the Latin name right at this moment."

My birding hadn't come as far as my tree identification. I could distinguish the larger birds, such as bald eagles, red-tailed hawks, and ospreys, but I grouped all birds less than five inches into the category of "small birds less than five inches." So I added a birding guide to my ever growing library and learned the bird in question was a tufted titmouse.

After helping Boomer with his tree species, the two of us stopped in Hardwick for a lunch on our way to the cabin. Each time our young, attractive waitress brought something to our table, I took a stab at small talk. When I asked her where she lived, I thought she said: "On my Daddy's big farm."

"How big is it?" I asked.

"How big is what?"

"The farm."

"It's not big at all. Why do you ask?"

"Because you said it was."

"Said what?"

"You said it was a big farm."

"No, I didn't."

I turned to Boomer, "Didn't she say she lived on a big farm?"

Boomer had a stupid grin on his face and was struggling to keep himself composed. "I believe," said Boomer, with great fanfare, "that the lady said she lived on her Daddy's *pig* farm."

I turned bright red. The waitress looked at me like I was a moron and stalked off.

A tear rolled down Boomer's cheek and he covered his face with his hands. I knew he was about to burst out laughing. He peeked out at me, managed to control himself for a moment, and whispered, "I gotta get out of here; I gotta get back to Daddy's pig farm." And then he left me sitting there.

After our camping and fishing trip along the Lamoille, Boomer and I spent the next night at the cabin, but the next day he had to return to work, while I stayed for another couple of days. I spent one afternoon on a long hike into the hills, and I tried my deer call that's meant to mimic a lost or hurt fawn. By blowing softly into the call, which looks like a large whistle, a kind of bleating sound is emitted, similar to the sound a sheep might make. Ten minutes later I saw movement in the woods. A doe was cautiously making its way toward me. Behind her was another, smaller deer, perhaps another doe or a fawn. Both deer paused several hundred yards away, so I gave one very soft bleat to bring them in closer. The larger deer immediately pinpointed my location and came directly at me. When it got to about twenty-five feet from me, it just stood and stared at me. When I didn't move, it seemed to become agitated and pawed the ground. Another minute went by and the deer snorted and pranced in place before retreating a bit.

Curiosity, agitation, or a maternal instinct to aid one of her own kind was more powerful than caution. Again the deer came toward me, this time to within ten or fifteen feet, where it swung its head and snorted again. My heart was beating a mile a minute. It was as if the contact brought out my primitive self, and the deer and I were the only living things in the world. For that brief moment we were connected, almost as if some type of energy was flowing between us. I felt I could understand the deer's confusion and understand its need to make contact with me and find out if I was friend or foe.

Along with the sense of wonder I felt, there was a twinge of fear from being so near the deer. Who knows how close the deer would have come, if I hadn't finally broke the spell by talking. I simply said "hello," and the deer bounded away.

I'm convinced it was the deer's maternal instinct that made it move so close, and believe it or not, I've experienced something similar with a creature that is usually frightened of everything. Former president Jimmy Carter once claimed that while fishing he was attacked by a rabbit, and the whole country had a good laugh. But count me as a believer. While at the cabin I once accidentally stepped on a baby rabbit in a field of clover. The baby let out a squeal, and from across the field I watched the mother rabbit come running. I moved a few feet away from the baby, but as the mother drew closer it was clear she was coming for me and not the baby. I ran. The rabbit chased me. I ran faster.

On the last day of this strange vacation, the natural world had one last surprise for me. I was fishing out on the pond in my canoe when from out of nowhere came a crack of thunder and a bolt of lighting. I paddled for everything I was worth, and another crash exploded just as I reached shore and started running up the hill. It was pouring now, and before the third bolt hit, I was given a split-second warning, because I actually felt the electricity in the air: a sizzling noise just before I saw the flash of lightning.

When I reached the safety of the cabin, I was shaking all over. As I was walking toward the fridge, the loudest crack of all erupted, and from the refrigerator a blue and white ball of light, about the size of a Ping-Pong ball, came flying out with a pop. It seemed as if this storm was determined to get me no matter where I ran.

I honestly thought the cabin was going to explode, so I switched off the circuit breaker to wait the storm out. Then a microburst of swirling wind swept across the hill, ripping branches from trees. I had just taken a half step out onto the porch to watch the wind, when I heard a loud snap and saw the top of a spruce tree come sailing down, smacking into the ground in an upright position just three feet from the cabin. (Later I examined the fallen treetop more closely and found that its broken trunk was embedded six inches into the ground.) It looked like a giant had just stuck a thirty-foot Christmas tree by the front door of the cabin. I felt like Dorothy in the *Wizard of Oz,* and I wouldn't have been surprised if a cow had gone flying by.

Next came the hail (the local meteorologist later describing it "as the size of Macadamia nuts"). The hail and wind shook the cabin and I sought refuge inside but away from the windows, thinking they might get blown in. After two minutes the hail was much smaller—about the size of pistachio nuts—so I took a peek out the door. Three inches of hailstones had piled up where they had rolled down the side of the A-frame. I smiled at the complete winter scene in June—the giant Christmas tree at the cabin door and the ground coated white.

The guest book entries from Boomer and I summed up that strange summer visit:

*Mike impressed me with his newfound tree identification skills, but he's got a long way to go when flirting with waitresses. He also should learn that you can't catch fish in quicksand.*

*Witnessed an incredible thunderstorm—I'm convinced that storm had my number, but I got lucky.*

# CHAPTER 10

# A CLOSER LOOK

*Remember what you have seen, because everything forgotten
returns to the circling winds.*
—NAVAJO WIND CHANT

*You can't be suspicious of a tree, or accuse a bird or squirrel
of subversion, or challenge the ideology of a violet.*
—HAL BORLAND

By my fifth year, I became intrigued by wildlife I'd rarely seen in
suburbia and even focused my attention on the smaller creatures
such as the luna moth. On the evening in June when I saw my
first luna moth, I thought my imagination had finally got the best
of me. Attracted to the porch light, the luna moth floated by
briefly, and because it was so big I initially thought it was more
mammal than moth. Then it circled back and landed on the door.
Upon closer inspection I could see that this was indeed a moth,
but one of such beauty that all other moths—and even butter-
flies—paled in comparison. An unusual light green color, almost
fluorescent, it had a wingspan of five inches. The hind wings
tapered into flowing tails, giving it an other-worldly appearance.

Since that first sighting I always consider it good luck when a
luna moth visits the cabin, and fireflies seem magical, too. How
can a bug have a light inside? Five chemicals residing in the bug's

abdomen are bonded together until a nerve stimulation releases another chemical, inorganic pyrophosphate, and when the bond breaks, light is the result. While that scientific approach explains the process, it doesn't touch on the human reaction to it, which for me is one of pure wonder.

This incredible light show takes place during the mating process. Fireflies communicate their intent through a series of signals, much the same way ships use signal lights and beacons. The male fireflies do most of the searching and flashing, and the interested females respond with flashes of their own. The odds are against the male, as they outnumber females by ten to one, so competition is fierce. Even worse, a few females intentionally mimic the females of different species in hopes of luring a male to them, not for mating, but for dinner.

The more I learn, the more I realize how complex the web of life is.

When I tried to tell people back in the office about the fireflies and luna moths, they politely nodded. Seeing those creatures during the quiet, dark nights at the cabin had an effect on me that might not have occurred had I seen them in suburbia. At the cabin I had the time to appreciate them, and without the street-lights to mar their magic they seemed nothing less than wood-land fairies. I quickly learned not to talk about these feelings to my roommates back in Boston or to the folks in the office; they thought I was odd enough spending so many weekends alone at the cabin.

I occasionally wondered if it was normal for someone to spend their free time alone watching bugs, bats, and birds from a secluded hilltop. It concerned me, but I felt blessed that I could derive such enjoyment from such simple pleasures. I could sense a subtle change in myself. I was starting to appreciate the little things, finding miracles in nature and not needing my regular daily stimuli of newspapers, TV, and pointless conversation. Maybe this was just another outcome of attending the "University of the Wilderness."

I never saw myself as a hermit; I was around people all week. I always had the option to spend weekends with friends, or as Robert Frost said, "When I tired of trees I seek again mankind."

The porcupines had long since been gone from the privy and it was safe. In fact, porcupines were becoming downright scarce compared to the first couple years when I would frequently see one up in a tree contentedly nipping buds. I wondered why they left; I hadn't cut any of the hemlock trees they love to feed on, and no dogs were around to harass them. For that matter, I figured nothing could really worry the porcupines, because nothing could harm them, but I was wrong.

The fisher, a member of the weasel family (about twice as large as a martin or roughly the same size as a raccoon), deliberately hunts the porcupine. After being reintroduced to the region in an effort to curb the numbers of porcupines, fisher populations have been steadily climbing during the last twenty years, and they were the reason I'd been seeing fewer porcupines. I saw a fisher (usually called "fisher cats" in the north country) near the Lamoille River, and it was like looking into the eyes of the wilderness itself. The fisher glared at me with coal-black eyes, almost in a challenge. Its coat was a glossy brownish-black, and it had rounded ears on top of a wedge-shaped head. It then ran partway up a tree before stopping and staring again with the fierce look of a true predator.

My brother Bob had a similar experience while sitting on the steps of the cabin porch. A fisher walked up the dirt lane, not noticing Bob until it was ten feet away. It stopped and stared before moving off toward the pond. In the guest book Bob wrote:

*What an experience, a sleek-looking fisher came within a few feet of me, and appeared to be annoyed that I was sitting on the cabin steps before it headed down the hill.*

I doubt there's another animal in the eastern U.S.—except perhaps a bear—that would willingly tangle with a fisher; a fox would be no match and a coyote might not survive. The only animal that rivals the fisher in ferocity, pound for pound, is the wolverine, whose range in the northeast is limited to northern Canada.

After being trapped to the point of extirpation in the mid-1800s, the fisher has made a steady comeback through a reintroduction program started in 1959 by Vermont wildlife biologists. Trappers in the seventeenth century received the princely sum of up to $350 for fisher sable. People of that time were happy to be rid of the fisher, as their ferocity was translated to a human quality of "evil" (which, in my opinion, only humans possess). Fishers were credited with carrying off large dogs and even small children. Neither is true, of course, but fishers will easily make a meal out of the household cat.

The method a fisher uses to kill a porcupine is not pleasant. It circles its prey and with lightning-fast moves strikes at the porcupine's head. Eventually the porcupine slows down due to fatigue and loss of blood, and the fisher moves in for the kill. Should the porcupine seek refuge in a tree, the fisher is agile enough to stay right with it, forcing the porcupine to the tip of the branch. Then the fisher closes in on the porcupine, forcing it to fall to the ground, where the deadly circling process is repeated. The fisher continues this attack until it sees an opening to charge on the porcupine's unprotected belly. The fisher can even withstand a few quills; they cause no festering or swelling, often passing right through the fisher's digestive track.

In the few short years I had owned the cabin, I witnessed a change in the fortunes of much of the North Woods wildlife, such as the expansion of moose and fishers and the decline of brook trout and woodcocks. Some species were replacing others, taking over their range, while others reestablished themselves because of changing habitats. (In the mid-nineteenth century, New England was only 20 percent forested due to logging and the creation of new pastures, but since that time farmland has been reverting to forest and today approximately 80 percent of land is forested.) Newcomers have arrived as well, such as the coyote, filling the niche vacated by the demise of the wolf at the turn of the twentieth century and taking advantage of the abundance of small game.

When I went to Saint Michael's College outside Burlington, Vermont, in the mid-1970s, I never saw a single coyote in my four years of living and hiking in the region. By the time I bought my cabin in 1978, I began to see one or two each year, usually while out hiking or driving, and thought how much they looked like sleek German shepherds. They usually move with a long, loping stride, and when the need arises they can break into a run of thirty miles per hour.

The coyote moved into the northeast probably by way of Canada starting in the late-1940s, and many experts think they interbred with wolves, because the ones here are larger than their western cousins. I've heard some people theorize that the eastern coyote is actually part dog, "a coy-dog," but Peter Marchand, author of *North Woods,* explains the evidence shows this to be untrue, based on analysis of crossbreeding siblings captured from the same litter of eastern coyotes. When the siblings produced a litter of pups they were uniform, and genetically this can only happen if the parents are of the same breed. If the parents are offspring of a coyote and a dog, they would produce some pups that look like a pure coyote and some that look like the domestic dog. Biologists also point out that male eastern coyotes help care for their young, while domestic dogs do not.

Coyotes are opportunistic feeders; I've seen two follow behind a tractor mowing hay, jumping on the displaced mice. Nobody minds the coyote eating mice, but mention the coyote to some deer hunters and you're in for a long harangue about the evils of this sly predator. The claim, however, that coyotes have caused a drop in deer populations is dubious, say most wildlife biologists. Coyotes will take a sick deer, fawn, or yearling, but running down a full-grown healthy deer would be rare. More than likely, it's free-running domestic dogs that will chase the deer for miles, often forcing it out onto ice, where the exhausted deer breaks a leg. The coyote will then move in for a free meal and get the blame for the killing. A coyote wouldn't chase a deer for miles through the woods the way a pack of well-fed dogs would. The coyote could actually be the one to weaken and die if it practiced going after prey that invariably escaped, whereas the domestic dog can head on home for a good meal.

Despite the experts' belief that coyotes don't actively hunt healthy deer, they are definitely cunning predators on par with the fisher. They are deadly hunters when targeting rabbits, snowshoe

hares, ground-nesting birds, and even house cats. One police officer in the Massachusetts town I currently live in told me that he
once came upon a coyote den and found five cat collars strewn
around the opening. Coyotes have also taken sheep and small
dogs, and suburbanites cry foul when their beloved pet is carried
off by a mother coyote to feed her young. I think we all need to
realize that when our pets are outside, they have entered the
realm of the natural world and can become part of the food
chain, with coyotes a notch above dogs and cats.

Perceptions, however, are hard to change. One friend near the
cabin shot a coyote and hung its head on his shed, saying, "That's
one less sly, dirty bastard ruining the woods."

Maybe I'm more sympathetic to the coyote because I'm not a
deer hunter or livestock owner, and I actually find the animal
quite graceful. Observing a coyote crossing a field near the cabin,
I was struck by its intelligent face when it glanced back at me. It's
funny how my neighbor describes the coyote as sly, while I would
call the same attribute intelligence.

Coyote attacks on humans are almost unheard of in the east,
and in my years of following the expansion of coyotes, the only
attack I can recall happened on Cape Cod. This particular coyote
had become habituated to being around people, going through
garbage and probably dining on house cats at night. When it saw
a three-year-old boy playing in his yard, the coyote charged and
began to drag the boy off. Fortunately the boy's mother was nearby and she drove the coyote away.

To solve such problems in the future, we might take a page
from a bear control program initiated in Colorado. Black bears in
the area were invading homes and prowling neighborhoods,
looking for seed at bird feeders and for garbage left outside. The
bears became bolder and bolder when they realized there was
nothing to fear from humans.

The program, called "Bear Spanking," changed the bears'
behavior when approaching areas where humans live. The animal
control officer in essence became the dominant bear, or the alpha
male, showing them that this was *his* territory, not theirs. First,
offending bears were driven off with pepper spray and most
never returned, although if that technique was not enough to

deter a particularly bold bear, the next step was a cherry bomb or a flare fired at the bear. If further action was needed, a rubber bullet was fired at the bear. The program worked wonders; bears began to fear humans and left town.

Although it has not been tried, the same concept would probably work for coyotes. If a particular coyote is showing bolder and bolder behavior, it's probably because food is easy to obtain near humans and humans don't pose a threat. The coyote would think otherwise if it associated humans with danger.

Coyotes, bears, and fishers may be at the top of the food chain, but it was a raccoon that won the honors of the boldest creature at the cabin. While fishing one evening, I had just laid my catch directly behind me when I heard a rustling in the woods and a pair of red eyes peered out from the bushes. Apparently the scent of the fish attracted the raccoon, but its fear of humans kept it from coming any closer. It ducked back into the brush and I assumed it wandered off, when in actuality it was lying in ambush. As the evening grew darker and I moved a few feet away for another cast, the raccoon made its move. I turned just in time to see the raccoon pick up my trout and run off. I shouted and started after it, but the masked bandit kept going and, without looking back, was gone, making a clean getaway with my fish!

Another thief raided me that same summer when Cogs joined me for a weekend at the cabin, each of us trying to catch the largest bass. On the first day of the weekend, the competition was not going my way; Cogs caught and released a two-and-a-half-pound smallmouth, and I had a four-inch sunfish. It didn't help that the next morning I overslept and found Cogs had already left in the canoe.

Standing on the dock, I made a few halfhearted casts, never expecting to catch anything. Luck was with me, however, and I landed a nice four-pound smallmouth. I tied the fish to a stringer and placed it in the water, attaching the other end to the dock so that the fish could swim around until Cogs came back. I went back to the cabin to enjoy a big breakfast, secure in the knowledge that I'd won the competition. A few minutes later, when I heard Cogs paddle up to the dock, I ran down and announced that the competition was over. I instructed Cogs to close his eyes and went to pull up the fish.

At the end of the stringer all that was left was the head of the smallmouth. Something had eaten the entire body in a span of just fifteen minutes.

In a deadpan voice Cogs said, "Fish heads don't count. I believe you have forfeited the competition."

I never figured out what ate my prized smallmouth, although a good bet would be a snapping turtle or otter. Not learning from mistakes, a similar occurrence happened years later. Maybe it served me right for fishing competitively rather than for enjoyment.

Snappers may take our fish, but at least they don't come after us. Compared to other areas of the country, New England is a relatively benign place when it comes to what can harm you in the great outdoors. I never think twice about jumping in a river, lake, or pond; the worst that can happen is I might surface with a leech attached to my body. Even midnight skinny-dipping doesn't pose a problem. Not so, however, when you head to the Deep South, where a jump in the lake may bring you eye to eye with an alligator or cottonmouth.

New England is tame by comparison. We have no alligators or crocodiles, and the only poisonous snakes that live here—the timber rattlesnake and the copperhead—are so rare I've never seen either in all my years of hiking. In fact, both snakes are also considered endangered and it is illegal to harass or harm them. Although both the rattlesnake and copperhead have crossbands, that is not enough to make an identification, because several other snakes have similar markings. One sure way to know if a snake is poisonous is by observing its head. If its head is triangular as opposed to oval, it's poisonous.*

---

*Of course, if you're close enough to distinguish the shape of a snake's head, you could be congratulating yourself for this discovery while the venom races through your body.

Although I now walk the woods without fearing wildlife and swim without concern for whatever else lives in the water, I've certainly seen some strange creatures that gave me a scare when first encountered. Take the case of the "Incident on the Raft," as Cogs refers to it.

One spring Cogs and I constructed a raft and anchored it out in the pond about thirty feet from shore. Although with the two of us on it, it barely floated above the waterline, we were immensely proud of our achievement. That summer we spent countless hours napping, sunning, and just talking as we lay on the raft. One sultry summer afternoon we languidly swam out to the raft and climbed up for a little sun. We were both lying with our eyes closed, letting the heat and humidity embrace us, knowing we could cool off anytime we wanted by just rolling off the raft.

"What do you say we swim to the road and back?" asked Cogs.

"Too tired. I'm happy right here."

Cogs slowly eased himself up into a sitting position. That's when he saw THE THING.

"Oh my God," he whispered, "don't move a muscle."

I was still half asleep, not even sure if I heard him correctly. "Don't what?"

"Do exactly as I tell you. Carefully roll to your left."

I could hear the alarm in his voice. Ignoring his instructions, I opened my eyes and quickly sat up.

Cogs screamed, "Look out! By your knee!"

I felt something brush against my leg and screamed. The largest, fattest, ugliest spider in the world was walking ever so slowly along the inside edge of my leg. I sprang up and hurled myself into the lake.

When I surfaced, Cogs was sitting on the raft as still as a statue, although I could barely see him without my glasses on.

"How can you sit there?" I screamed at Cogs.

"Because I don't know where it is. When you jumped, it disappeared."

I was calming down and paddled closer to the raft so I could see Cogs clearly. "That thing was as big as a mouse. It had to be two inches across. It even had brown fur on its legs."

As I looked at Cogs, it appeared a big smile was spreading across his face, so I eased a bit closer to be certain. Yes, he was smiling.

"Mikey," Cogs said in a singsong voice, "look behind you."

A chill went up my spine as I turned in the water. Less than three feet away was, not one, but three giant spiders, standing—and I do mean standing, not floating—on the water's surface. We were eyeballs to eyeballs.

Cogs stood up on the raft for a better view, and I swear, yet *another* spider came out from under the raft and started scurrying toward me. These things could really move on top of the water, with all eight legs supporting their bodies. I had seen enough and swam to shore for all I was worth.

Aren't spiders supposed to be in dusty old corners spinning intricate webs? Not all of them, I later found out. What we had seen was a fishing spider, a member of the nursery web family of spiders. In *The World of Spiders,* author Adrienne Mason explains that they resemble the land-based wolf spider in general appearance but are much larger. "The fishing spider is a specialist that sits motionless on the surface of water, waiting for a passing fish or insect. Some may even use the end of their legs as a lure." Their legs also detect motion in the water such as a struggling insect, and they then capture their prey with their strong jaws and venom.

At first I wasn't wild about a whole colony of these spiders living under my raft, but over the course of the next few years, I reached a kind of truce with the spiders. They rarely came onto my side of the raft if I didn't rock it too much, and they didn't seem all that aggressive the few times I did see them, usually heading away from me rather than toward me. Another reason for my acceptance was a fact I stumbled across in my spider research that made fishing spiders seem as frightening as baby kittens. Black widow spiders live in the northeast. And get this—they often inhabit outhouses.

I read this in an interesting nature book titled *Blood Brook,* by Ted Levin, who found black widow spiders on his property in Vermont. While the black widow Levin found was under a rock, he points out they are partial to outhouses, since "they fashion webs across privy seats to snare pupating flies that rise from the festering mounds of manure below. . . . A California survey of black widow bites indicates that women are most often bitten on the hip or buttocks, men on the tip of the penis." Yikes.

After digesting that little nugget of newfound knowledge, I felt I was back to where I had been the first summer I owned the cabin: ready to hand the keys over to the first taker. Before I gave into my fear, I had to make sure Levin was correct, so I read *The Encyclopedia of Dangerous Insects.* If I was looking for some soothing words to lessen my anxiety, I was wrong. I learned that the black widow's venom is fifteen times more potent than the venom of a rattlesnake, and one survivor of a black widow bite endured what he described as "huge tidal waves" of excruciating pain. Not only did the book confirm that black widows can extend their range into the northern United States, but it also reiterated what Levin said about outhouses. The book explains that no one really needs to worry about black widows except the poor sap who still uses an outhouse. "The introduction of modern plumbing has significantly reduced the incidence of black widow envenomizations; nearly half the black widow bites reported in medical literature during the first four decades of this century were inflicted by spiders lurking under outdoor lavatory seats. Avoid darkened corners of attics, barns, basements, abandoned buildings—and outhouses."

I'm glad to have slowed down enough to notice all these neighbors, but when I read about the black widows, part of me shouted, "Bring back the porcupines!"

*I've seen a lot of strange things, but the spider walking on the water chasing Toug takes the cake. (Cogs)*

# CHAPTER 11

# THE WONDERS OF THE POND

*A lake is the landscape's most beautiful and expressive feature.*
*It is the earth's eye; looking into which the beholder measures*
*the depth of his own nature.*
—HENRY DAVID THOREAU, *WALDEN*

Despite my encounter with the fishing spiders, I loved my pond like it was a friend. I never took it for granted but gave thanks for its seclusion, its clean waters, and for the therapeutic powers I believed it had. Its small size—about twenty-five acres—is actually a blessing. Motorboats are not a worry, because the pond is simply not large enough, and even canoes and kayaks are rarely on the water. The absence of many boaters has helped keep the pond free of exotic plants such as milfoil and water chestnut that plague so many larger lakes. These invasive plants can choke a lake with explosive growth, and they are often introduced to new bodies of water via the propellers of trailered boats.

There are no ostentatious trophy homes looming over the pond's waters, no huge windows of glass to steal its reflection, and no manicured lawns slopping to the shoreline. Of the five cabins that have land abutting the pond, only one can be seen from the water, while the rest, like mine, are set far back from the shoreline, hidden in the woods. Standing like sentinels, the trees along the shoreline help keep its waters pure, and there have been no algae blooms caused by nutrients leaching into the water.

Each season, I monitored the pond's health by employing the primitive technique of using my feet. So long as my toes felt the rough texture of submerged rocks rather than a "fuzzy" slime from algae, I felt confident that man-made nutrients were not present. My other crude test was visual. I'd check the pond's clarity, noting that from my dock I could always look out and see to a depth of six feet. These tests assured me the hazards I could see and feel were not present, but I could only hope the unseen pollutants—such as acidity or mercury introduced by rain—were not hurting the pond's health.

During the summer of my fifth year at the cabin, I decided to increase my knowledge of the pond by conducting a "pond inventory." This consisted of circling the pond on an old air mattress, paddling as silently as possible, and taking along a mask and snorkel and a notebook wrapped in a plastic bag to record what I saw (and from which I now refer to as I write). My goal was to discover as much as I could about the pond's ecosystem and to use the information as a baseline from which to monitor changes over the years. On a morning in early July I set out on my little mattress, first paddling out to the pond's center, where I took in the scene, noting that no matter which direction I faced, only two colors were visible. Overhead the sky was cobalt blue without a trace of clouds. The encircling hills formed an intimate ring of green, with foliage so thick the limbs and trunks of trees were obscured. The pond itself seemed to borrow the hues from both sky and hills, creating its own blue-green tone. Occasionally a breeze rippled the surface of the water, making it sparkle in the sunshine.

I began paddling in a counterclockwise direction, heading close to the shore, where tree roots, like an owl's talons, gripped boulders and jagged edges of slate. Most of the trees on this north-facing shore are hemlock and spruce, with one large white pine towering above. Two trees stood with bare limbs, dead from beavers gnawing around their trunk, shavings lying in mute testament to the beavers' half-finished work.

Cupping my hands around my eyes, I lowered my head to the water and peered below. I recalled how years earlier my friend Dale had done the same thing and I had quietly snorkeled up so we were suddenly face to face. Now I understood why he panicked.

It's so peaceful looking down into the pond's depth, it's easy to daydream, and the last thing you expect is a head popping up.

Being the only human on the pond, I didn't have to worry about practical jokes, but instead could watch the pond's bottom as if enjoying a movie. Very little plant life grows in the shade of the shore trees, and I watched a smallmouth bass fin in place then glide to deeper water as the shadow of the mattress passed by. Farther along, a pumpkinseed hovered above a bed it had scooped out of gravel, showing little concern as I approached. Earlier in the year, the bass would have been guarding their own spawning beds, and I learned that that was the time to catch them, when they struck a lure instinctively to protect their beds rather than to feed.

Wanting to get a close-up view of the pumpkinseed, I put on my mask and snorkel then eased off the raft and into the pond's bracing water. I dove down, cruising by the mottled orange and blue-green pumpkinseed, which eyed me warily but did not yield its position. I followed the sloping shoreline down to deeper water. The water at the top four or five feet was cool, but nothing like the bone-numbing icy layer below, where the springs feed the pond. Back on the surface, I climbed up on the mattress and paddled quickly to reach a section of water that was not shaded.

Is there anything so wonderful as a cool swim and then a return to sunshine? How alive I felt. Not only did my skin tingle, but all my other senses seemed to have awakened too, and I could actually smell that wonderful scent of fresh water, of life itself. Where a small island and a rocky point formed a miniature cove, I paddled to the sunny side and breathed deeply, enjoying the faint, dank scent of earth and evergreen, catching the sweet whiff of the ferns.

The tranquility I relished from the calming effect of water has been felt by many others, from Thoreau referring to his Walden Pond as "liquid joy," to Louise Dickinson Rich writing about her beloved "B Pond" in *We Took to the Woods*. "There is that feeling," wrote Rich, "of remoteness and calm and timelessness about it that makes the scramble of ordinary life seem like a half-forgotten and completely pointless dream." Timelessness is an apt description; it's as if life itself came out of the fertile ooze along the margin of the pond just yesterday.

As I pushed back to deeper water, a flash of movement on shore caught my eye. A mink was frozen in mid-step, and in its mouth was a frog. Apparently the mink had just captured its prey and was returning toward its den when it saw me. It was clear the mink wanted to continue along the shoreline, but its path would take it directly in front of me as I floated not ten feet away. Perhaps it didn't know what to make of this object on the water, because it seemed to study the situation before making a decision. In a burst of speed it raced across and around the rocky shoreline in front of me and darted into a four-inch opening under a tree root.

Frogs are only one of many creatures a mink will eat. It is an opportunistic carnivore, feeding on snakes, crayfish, fish, waterfowl and their eggs, insects, mice, and cottontails. The mink, however, is not a large predator, and it in turn is prey to animals farther up the food chain, such as bobcats, great horned owls, coyotes, fishers, and foxes. While the pond may have appeared serene to me, seeing the mink with the frog reminded me that these waters and shoreline are a food factory, where life and death dramas are played out each day and night.

As I paddled by the east end of the pond where the gravel road passes by, I recalled other wildlife surprises I've had here. A fox once trotted down the road toward me as I was quietly fishing from shore. Like the mink, the fox had something in its mouth too, but its catch was much larger. At first I couldn't tell what it was, but soon recognized the fox was carrying the hind leg of a deer. When the fox saw me, it dashed into the woods, somehow keeping a tight grip on the big leg. I wondered if the fox had come upon a dead deer and carried off the leg or if the fox had found an injured deer and killed it.

And with a pang of guilt I also remembered the water snake I had killed here. Now, floating on my raft and enjoying the pond with all its diversity, it seemed like the incident of the snake with the frog, and the boy hollering for me to do something had occurred in a different lifetime, but in fact it was just five years ago.

The northeast section of the pond has a shallow, weedy area that extends forty feet, with a depth averaging only three to four feet. I've always called this the pickerel patch because of the many pickerel that swim through these weeds, probably to launch their ambushes on smaller fish. With a mouth of jagged teeth, long narrow jaws, and a sleek body, the pickerel is the barracuda of freshwater fish. Unlike so many other fish that feed at night, the pickerel is active all day, and an angler who is having a slow day would do well to visit the pickerel patch and cast a minnow lure into a weedy opening. If the lure has a touch of red painted on it, all the better, because when a pickerel sees red it acts like an enraged bull and charges.

I always fish for pickerel using top-water lures, and more than once I've caught them in as little as five inches of water. The visual aspect of seeing the pickerel race toward my plug before slamming it always gets my heart pounding, even when the fish is just a foot long. Pickerel can grow to a length of thirty-one inches, but the biggest one I've caught on the pond was seventeen inches. I had a heck of a time getting the lure out of its long, flat snout, and it must have taken me three minutes. They are hardy fish, however, and when I released it, the pickerel surprised me by recovering immediately and rocketing away like a torpedo.

A small stream enters the pickerel patch through a tangled meadow of alders, reeds, marsh grass, and cattails. It seems like the perfect place for muskrats, with their tremendous appetite for aquatic plants, but I've never seen one. I wonder if that's because beavers have laid claim to the marsh and have driven any muskrats away. But this is just a personal theory, for while the beavers and muskrats prefer the same habitat, their diets are different and they really are not competitors for food. The muskrat primarily eats cattails, sedges, arrowheads, bulrushes, and occasionally clams, mussels, snails, and fish. Trees are the beaver's main source of food—particularly the cambium bark, leaves, and buds—and among their favorite species are alders, willows, and cottonwoods.

The beaver lodge on my pond is situated at the edge of the sedge meadow, and the underwater canal to the lodge was visible from my raft. The lodge is comprised of large branches, logs, and mud compacted so tightly it resembles a wigwam, complete with small bushes growing from its top, which extends five feet above the water. The living compartment is up near the top, and the lodge may have more than one underwater entrance. Alder, maple, and poplar are used in the construction of the lodge, so besides the branches the beaver drags into the lodge for food, it can also eat part of the lodge itself if it gets desperate during the winter. I always thought the beavers that live along rivers were a different subspecies, but they are the exact same animal. They don't need a lodge, because they can easily make a burrow in the riverbank with an underwater entrance.

When I first bought the cabin, I had no idea there were beavers in the pond, but I found out in a hurry. I was sitting on the shore, soaking up the sun, when the peace was shattered by a booming "thwack" on the water. My first thought was that someone had thrown a large rock into the water, so I jumped up and looked behind me in the woods. Then the thwack sounded again, and I turned just in time to see the beaver dive below the surface. In retrospect this surprise greeting between the beaver and me was a good thing because it helped prepare me for our next encounter, which was also initiated by the beaver. Our second visit occurred when I was taking a swim and the beaver again scared the life out of me, surfacing from under water within six or seven feet of where I was paddling. Without my glasses on, I wasn't sure what it was and every wild thought imaginable went through my mind. Was it the giant head of a snake or snapping turtle, or a prehistoric monster that had survived in my pond from the age of the dinosaur? Call me crazy, but talk to me after something pops up next to you in the water and you can't see clearly.

Once I realized it was a beaver I became curious, although I must admit I wondered what its intentions were. The beaver wasn't sure about me either, because it swam in a circle around me and with each circling pass it came a little closer. When it was within three feet and we were looking into each other's eyes, I splashed water on it. The beaver immediately dove, and for a

second I wondered if it was angry enough to attack, but instead
it surfaced a good twenty feet away. It looked back at me and
slapped its tail for good measure.

Seeing a beaver so close made me realize just how large
America's biggest rodent is. They are typically about forty pounds
and forty-five inches long including the tail, but I swear the one
that lives in my pond is much larger. And it may not be my imagination, because a beaver's growth rate will continue as long as it
lives, and there have been several documented cases of beavers in
New England weighing more than eighty-five pounds! One would
think with that size, razor-sharp teeth, and jaws strong enough to
cut down trees, beavers could defend themselves against just
about any predator. But when cornered on land, they barely put
up a fight. Of course, at the time the beaver swam circles around
me, I had no idea what it was capable of doing.

In Vermont beavers are often unwelcome because of the flooding they cause when they dam a stream. One Vermonter, however, had a different take on the beaver, welcoming it. "If it weren't
for the beaver," he told me, "I'd never see the sky." When I asked
him what he meant, he said, "Around where I live, everything was
hemmed in by hills and trees. But the beaver showed up making
a dam and meadow that provided an unobscured view of the sky."
He had a point. The beaver was also welcomed by early trappers
for its thick, watertight fur and for its meat, which was especially
welcomed by French Catholics on meatless Fridays, because the
pope had classified the beaver as a fish! (That's understandable,
since the beaver's fifteen-inch-long tail has scales on it and they
can stay submerged for up to fifteen minutes.)

Man is not the only creature to benefit from the beaver.
Because beavers can create a whole new ecosystem, turning forest into wetlands, amphibians, mink, otters, muskrats, reptiles,
and a wide assortment of ducks all take advantage of the new
habitat. Great blue herons in particular benefit, utilizing the
standing dead trees in the beaver ponds as nesting sites. The
herons have a measure of protection there, because a predator
would have to swim out to the tree before climbing. It also pro-
vides the heron a 360-degree view of the area, not to mention a
place to fish right below the nest.

As I continued my circle of the pond, I rolled over on my back and paddled along the northern shore, watching the day's first cloud sail by the horizon, imagining that the pointed firs could pierce the fleece-topped cloud and cause it to rain. Mixed with the dark firs at the water's edge, a few tamaracks lightened the scene with their blue-green lacy branches. A kingfisher streaked out from under the tamaracks and cried out a penetrating rattle that echoed off the encircling hills.

Near the western shore, I recalled how I was fishing here with Cogs when out of frustration I declared, "This is my last cast in this stupid pond. It's fishless!" On my "last cast" a four-pound smallmouth bass struck. The irony wasn't lost, and we thought complaining could lead to more hits. For the rest of that weekend we tried the technique on all the nearby trout streams, and of course, caught nothing.

I put my mask and snorkel back on and stuck my face over the front of the raft, hoping to see more smallmouths. For the first ten minutes I saw nothing noteworthy, until a boulder moved. The boulder turned out to be an enormous snapping turtle that, alarmed by my raft, lifted itself off the pond's bottom and glided to deeper water. Dimensions are exaggerated when looking through a mask, but even taking that into account, this snapper's shell was at least two feet wide. I made a note not to mention this to Cogs or Boomer or I'd be in jeopardy of losing the only two guests that still came to the cabin. (Since that day, however, I've seen several large snappers in other bodies of water, including the crystal-clear lakes of Maine and the spring-fed kettle-hole ponds of Cape Cod. People generally associate snapping turtles with muddy rivers and small ponds, but they inhabit just about any lake or waterway, which is a good thing because they eat dead fish, helping to keep the water clean.)

When my circle was completed, I felt I understood the pond better, understanding how interconnected the health of the pond is with the creatures that live in it and along its shore, from the smallest insect to the mink, beaver, and heron. I considered how some people see a pond or a lake as nothing more than a playground, utilizing it in whatever way they see fit, without a thought to their impact. If those same people, however, took a morning float on the water, simply to observe and discover, they might be more appreciative. Such an experience might enlighten us to use our intelligence to protect rather than dominate.

I should have considered my pond study a success and called it a day. Instead I decided to push it a step further. I had read that John Muir once slept on a boulder in the middle of a river, so I figured I'd try spending that night sleeping on my dock.

That evening I laid a foam pad and sleeping bag on the dock. Then, over the area where my head would be, I erected a bug net by nailing two foot-long poles on either side of the dock to keep the net hanging just off my face. I also placed a rock on either side of me so that I wouldn't roll off and into the water—it's hard to swim in a sleeping bag. . . .

I lay down listening to bullfrogs and the occasional splash of a fish. A half-moon rose, casting strange light on scattered clouds. When the cloud cover parted in the northern sky, the Big Dipper shone so brightly I could almost reach out and pull it in for a drink.

There was no breeze, but only the puffs of cool, dank air from the pond. It crossed my mind that I had seen bear scat by my dock last year, but I figured a bear would catch my scent and steer clear tonight. Surprisingly, I fell asleep quickly, listening to the call of a snipe on the hill and an owl up on the other side of the pond. Later, when I got up to pee and went to put my shoes on, my foot felt the squishy body of two slugs that had crawled into my sneakers. I picked one out and, without thinking, dropped it into the pond. Two seconds later the water broke where a fish came up and grabbed the slug. I tossed the second slug up into the woods, patting myself on the back for saving its life.

When I lay back down the trouble started. A whirling, fluttering noise just above my face made me freeze. As quickly as it came the noise stopped, and I tried to relax, closing my eyes. Then it came again, closer, just an inch or two from my head. I kept my eyes open, but when the noise came a third time, from a different direction, I couldn't see anything in darkness. Yet another whirling sound came, and this time I sat up and the thing hit the bug netting. I panicked, tearing at the netting like a fly writhing in a spider's web. I tried to stand, forgetting my legs were trapped in the mummy bag, and almost fell off the dock. On my back I twisted like a snake, not knowing if the thing was still in the netting. Then I heard a plop in the water next to the dock, and I realized I'd just knocked one of my shoes—with my glasses in it—into the water.

Finally, I lay still, knowing I was making the problem worse. I half expected the thing that hit the net to crawl over my face, but nothing happened. Another whirling sound passed by, and I now figured there were bats all around me. I forced myself to carefully get the net off and extract my legs from my sleeping bag. I crawled to the shore side of the dock and groped for my flashlight. Then I aimed the light down into the water and located my sneaker. Taking off my sweatpants, I eased into the water, crouching to my armpits to reach my sneaker. Fortunately, my glasses were inside.

Looking out on the pond I noticed the first hint of gray dawn revealing itself in layers of mist floating like ghosts above the water. The bats gave me a wider berth, and I decided to just sit still on the dock and watch a pond sunrise. The first soft birdsongs came drifting down the hill from the direction of the cabin.

A half hour later the first streaks of pink from the rising sun appeared. Gazing out at the water I was treated to the sight of a great blue heron in flight, gliding through the mist, neck crooked inward, feet trailing behind. I was almost glad the bats woke me up. I gathered my gear and started the hike up to the cabin for a cup of coffee. On the way up, a deer, its coat a rich russet, bolted past me then paused to look back. With its flag up and its ears craned forward, the deer and I looked at each other before it bounded into the woods and I continued climbing the path, both of us starting a new day.

My guest book entries from that trip indicate my fondness for the pond, but warn others about sleeping on the dock:

*Like a particular grand old tree that a person can come to love, I feel the same about the pond.*

*Don't think I'll be sleeping on the dock for a long time. Future guests may want to give it a try, and thereafter the mice in the cabin will be a piece of cake compared to bats by the dock.*

# CHAPTER 12

# INTO THE KINGDOM AND BEYOND: GAME WARDENS, MOOSE, AND FINE LODGING

*Why should it stand so high at the shoulders? Why have so long a head? Why have no tail to speak of?*
—THOREAU DESCRIBING A MOOSE

Three weeks after my night of sleeping on the dock, I was back in Vermont for a few days of vacation to travel through the northern sections of New England. My plan was to spend the first night at the cabin and then slowly head northeast, stopping in Vermont's Northeast Kingdom, the northernmost tip of New Hampshire, and then into Maine, heading toward Moosehead Lake.

After proving I could sleep by the pond with no shelter, I felt I deserved a reward, and on this upcoming trip I planned to alternate camping with staying at bed-and-breakfasts or rental cabins. I figured staying in a vacation cabin would be a luxury compared to sleeping on the dock with the bats. Of course, I figured wrong. I should have known that when you stay at places that advertise their accommodations as "pleasantly rustic" or "best rates around" or "a real North Woods experience," you get what you pay for.

After spending an uneventful night at my cabin, I began my trip the next morning with no set itinerary except to fish for brook trout in waters along a series of dirt roads that went in the general direction I was headed. As dusk approached I had not traveled more than thirty miles as the crow flies, but probably three times that distance driving the roadways, and tramping another five or six miles while fishing. I was tuckered out from wading through streams and climbing along their banks and was looking forward to a great night's sleep. I glanced at my atlas, headed toward the nearest paved road, and when I reached the first town, pulled into a side lane that led to some rental cabins. The cabins were set back in a semicircle in an unmowed field, nestled in the shadows of a forested hill that towered behind them. There were no cars in front of any of the cabins, and that should have tipped me off that this wasn't exactly sought-after lodging, but I was tired and all I could think of was a cold beer from my cooler and fresh white sheets to stretch out on.

A dim light came from a dilapidated building where the word "office" had been hand painted on a weathered shingle. At least, I thought to myself, it didn't say Bates Motel, but I half expected Alfred Hitchcock to step from the gloom and say "Goot evening."

As I got out of the car, I took another look at the cabins and noted that two of them were leaning to the starboard side, as if about to capsize. I knocked on the office door and a middle-aged man appeared, with greasy black hair and the dark stubble of a beard. He was pleasant enough as we walked toward cabin number 5, but still I made a mental note to barricade my door after locking it.

My cabin was one of those that were leaning. The man struggled with the door as he unlocked it, then allowed me to go in first. A sticky substance caught my nose, and I swatted it away while the owner fumbled for the light.

"Geez," he joked, "guess I'll have to get a few more guests coming through to keep the cobwebs down."

Cobwebs were everywhere, and it was obvious no one had stayed there in weeks. My eyes gave the single room the once-over, noting that the mattress looked like it came from the Civil War and the sheets could have dated to the Revolution. The owner showed me a little kitchen area, and I saw two mousetraps set in each corner.

Since no other cars were parked in front of the other cabins, I assumed he put me in number 5 because it was in the best shape. I could only imagine what lived in the other cabins.

As if reading my thoughts, he said, "I'm in the process of sprucing up the place."

He had his work cut out for him. If I wanted cobwebs, mousetraps, and furniture from the Eisenhower years, I could have stayed at my own cabin.

"You're welcome to stop by for a little bourbon once you get settled. It's on the house." He was dead serious. "Someday," he continued, "I'd like to get a liquor license and have a little restaurant so the guests could eat here and enjoy the evening."

I did not stop by for bourbon. It took me a long while to get to sleep, maybe because I kept feeling like I'd slide off the right side of the bed, since the cabin leaned that way. I was thankful I did not have more than the single beer, because the bed could give a whole new meaning to the "spins" that follow overindulging. I wondered who had been the last guest to stay here and if he or she was buried out back. I could just picture the surprise on the faces of some newlyweds who made reservations for the "rustic charm of the cozy cabins in the Green Mountain State" and arrived here too late to find other lodging. Then again, maybe newlyweds would never even notice the tilting bed.

Surprisingly, however, once I did fall asleep I slept soundly without awakening until 8:00 A.M., which is something of a record for me. A full day of walking trout streams can do wonders—even for a poor sleeper.

"Leaving so soon?" the owner asked when I checked out.

I actually felt a bit sad for him. He was obviously just squeaking by and lonely for company.

"Be back in a minute," he said. He ducked out of the office and into his den, where I could see the picture on a black-and-white TV, a couple of old dogs lounging on the rug, and not much else. He brought me a cup of coffee along with a beer for himself. The coffee was good, and before I left I debated about giving him a few suggestions about how to attract more guests. Where to start?

Now that it was daylight, I could see junk strewn about the yard and observed that the cabins hadn't been painted in years. In the end, I kept my suggestions to myself and turned the subject to fishing, and his eyes lit up. The more we talked, the more he hinted that he'd like to join me for the fishing trip. I remembered that I was on vacation and made my escape, wondering how this simple man got in the wrong business.

I spent the next few hours fishing and driving through Vermont's Northeast Kingdom, eventually stopping at a campground by Lake Willoughby, one of the most striking bodies of water I've ever seen. This long, narrow-shaped lake lies between Mount Hoar and Mount Pisgah, both of which have cliffs dropping right down to the water's edge, giving Willoughby the look of a Norwegian fjord. When I arrived, the tops of the mountains were shrouded in fog, giving them an eerie look.

Lake Willoughby is one of the deepest lakes in New England, and there have been rumors that a serpent swims in its 308-foot depths, similar to the one alleged to live in Lake Champlain. Sightings in Lake Willoughby go as far back as 1868. The Saint Johnsbury, Vermont, *Caledonian-Record* reported that a boy killed a snakelike creature a bit larger than your average water snake. Referring to the boy, the paper said, "Rushing boldly upon the monster he severed the body with a sickle. The two pieces were found to be 23 feet."

The Lake Willoughby sightings are few and far between compared to the Lake Champlain monster, dubbed "Champ." The alleged Champ is supposed to be a dinosaur/Loch Ness monster type of creature, with a long neck and a small head. There have been hundreds of reports, many from the 1990s. One viewer said the monster "was approximately 15 feet long with humps." Another witness described its head as looking like "a snail's head without the antennae." Not the kind of creature that strikes fear in your heart.

However, one sighting—which I actually believe—does make me think twice about taking a dip in lakes like Champlain and Willoughby. The viewer chronicles a creature more fishlike than the Loch Ness variety, but this was no ordinary fish and the witness is no ordinary traveler. The witness I am referring to is Samuel de Champlain, the lake's namesake. In 1609 Champlain joined a group of allied Indians on a mission to attack the Iroquois. To reach the enemy they had to paddle birch-bark canoes south on Lake Champlain, which at that time was a kind of no-man's-land separating the Iroquois Nation from the Algonquin tribes to the east. While on the northern end of the lake, Champlain recorded the description of the strange creature.

> There is also a great abundance of fish, of many varieties: among others, one called by the savages of the country Chaousarous, which varies in length, the largest being, as the people told me, eight or ten feet long. I saw some five feet long, which were as large as my thigh: the head being as big as my two fists, with a snout two feet and a half long, and double row of very sharp and dangerous teeth. Its body is, in shape, much like that of a pike: but it is armed with scales so strong that a poniard could not pierce them. Its color is silver-gray. The extremity of its snout is like that of swine. This fish makes war on all others in the lakes and rivers and possesses, as these people assure me, a wonderful instinct; which is, that when it wants to catch any birds, it goes among the rushes or reeds bordering the lake in many places, keeping the beak out of water without budging, so that when the birds perch on his beak, imagining it a limb of a tree, it is so subtle that closing the jaws which it keeps half open, it draws the birds under water by the feet. The Indians gave me a head of it, which they prize highly saying, when they have a headache they let blood with the teeth of this fish at the seat of the pain which immediately goes away.

That night I camped near the southern end of Lake Willoughby, and my campsite was free of cobwebs and sloping floors. Everything was perfect—no bugs, a good campfire to read by, and those cool temperatures that make for great sleeping. Even my dreams were pleasant. I dreamed a giant two-humped creature slithered out of my pond and ate Boomer.

When dawn broke, a thin layer of mist hung over the lake, covering the water but not the tops of Mount Hoar and Pisgah, just the opposite of the evening before. I had a glimpse of a peregrine falcon high up on the cliffs, and I decided this was a lake worth visiting again.

I did come back the next spring and had an encounter with a porcupine that made me wonder if I would ever learn from past mistakes. I saw a porcupine in a large maple tree contentedly eating the buds off the ends of the branches. Wanting a photo, I climbed the tree and shimmied out on the same branch the porcupine was on. Now that I considered myself a novice naturalist, I was getting a little cocky with my recently acquired knowledge. Specifically, I figured I had nothing to fear from a porcupine, because they cannot throw their quills. I reckoned that as I straddled the branch and got up close for our photo shoot, the porcupine would get nervous and eventually go farther out on the limb. What I didn't reckon is that its nervousness would cause it to turn and want to get off the tree, which meant it would be coming directly at me. When I was just four feet from the porcupine, it did just that. It was a mad scramble off the tree, and I scraped every exposed piece of flesh on my body as I slid down with the porcupine right behind me. When I got off the tree I finally realized why the animal had reacted as it did. At the base of the tree was a hollow opening, and the porcupine quickly went inside and disappeared. Had I been half the naturalist I thought I was, I would have noticed both the opening and the porcupine scat that covered the adjacent ground before I climbed the tree.

Before I packed up my tent, I took a long walk along the shores of Lake Willoughby, thinking how rough and rugged this Northeast Kingdom section of Vermont looked. I stayed on the main road, not wanting to tackle the mountains alone, perhaps because I recently had read what happened to Rogers's Rangers here in 1759. During the French and Indian Wars, Major Robert Rogers, who commanded a group of Rangers in the Colonial Militia, led a surprise attack on an enemy Indian village. This was no ordinary raid, but an incredibly daring—some might say foolish—gamble. Major Rogers led his group of Rangers from their base at Crown Point, near the southern end of Lake Champlain, and boated up the lake to the bay at the Missisquoi River. The Rangers then trekked through the uncharted wilds of northern Vermont and into Canada, where they attacked and wiped out the Indian village. The real fun began after the raid, when the Rangers had to get back to the nearest colonial outpost, which happened to be a couple hundred miles to the south at the fort at Number 4. From what I've gleaned from Rogers's journal, and from getting a peek at a privately owned map that Rogers was said to have drawn, it appears the Rangers passed right by Lake Willoughby. Although the Rangers were the hardiest of all the Colonial troops, it was the land itself rather than the French or the Indians that was their undoing on this return trip. The mountains, the cold, and—most importantly—the lack of food, weakened the men so that only a few survived.

You may recall the movie *Northwest Passage* directed by King Vidor, based on Kenneth Roberts's book of the same title. Spencer Tracy played Major Rogers and Robert Young played Langdon Towne, and both did a good job acting out the misery of the return march of the Rangers. It was the supporting character actors, however, that really caught my attention, especially the Ranger who, despite being utterly exhausted, carried a heavy sack presumably filled with loot from the Indian village. Later in the movie, the Ranger shows signs of going mad and one of the leaders decides to throw the loot away, only to find that the Ranger had been carrying around one of the heads of the enemy upon which he had been gnawing from time to time.

See what these woods can do to you?

When I packed my tent and finished admiring the mist, cliffs, and falcon at Lake Willoughby, I headed northeast to the headwaters of the Connecticut River, which offers some excellent fly-fishing. Pittsburg, New Hampshire, is the largest township in New Hampshire and the least populated, with most of the land forested and owned by International Paper Company. Just over the border in Canada, however, much of the land is cleared for fields and pasture with the little town of Chartiersville resting at a crossroads. I'll always remember Chartiersville because of its odd signs: the mysterious Magnetic Hill sign, the mysterious road sign, and the mysterious bar sign.

First the Magnetic Hill sign. This is located at the base of a hill where the road dips just before it starts climbing again. If you stop your car, turn off your engine, and shift into neutral, the forces of Magnetic Hill will pull your car back up the hill toward the U.S. side. Now, understand that your car does not go racing up the hill, but it does begin rolling for about thirty feet—a strange enough experience that I repeated the process five times. The Magnetic Hill sign says nothing about the cause of this phenomenon, but the name implies there is a magnetic force that overcomes gravity. Go up there and try it if you don't believe me.

And while you're there, take a look at two other signs and let me know what they are all about. One is a yellow road sign that shows a woman lying down in a bathing suit or leotard. She is on her back and her knees are bent. At first I thought it was a woman in labor and assumed there might be a hospital about. Then I surmised the woman was sunbathing, and I figured there was a lake with a beach close by. If I knew French, I'd have the correct answer, because there were some French words beneath the sign. One of them said "enfant," so maybe my first guess about a woman in labor was correct. The sign will remain a mystery for me and others who cannot read French, but for those who understand the language, here is what it said: "Attention A Nos Enfants C'est Peut-Etre Le Votre."

The other sign I saw on that trip was equally strange. This one was outside of a bar. There were actually two signs announcing this was a "bar salon" and each displayed a large five-foot-by-four-foot cartoon-style drawing. One of the drawings, on the left side of the bar entrance door, made sense to me. It showed Wilma and Fred Flintstone dancing, and in the background were a couple of drinks with straws in them. I figured that was a nice, cute way to advertise that people who stopped in this bar would have a good time. But it was the drawing on the right side of the door that had me worried, particularly if it too was depicting what was happening inside the bar. It is hard to explain what the drawing was about without being too graphic, so I'll just get right to the point. It showed a moose humping a donkey. The moose looked happy, with tongue out and eyes rolled back. The donkey, judging by the grimace on its face, was not enjoying the romance. Beneath the picture was a simple greeting "Bienvenue, Welcome."

I pondered this picture for several minutes, trying to get up my courage to go in the bar. Some kids from town were hanging out in front of the lounge, and they were watching me stand there with smirks on their faces. I looked at them, then back at the sign, and opened my arms up with palms skyward, indicating I was confused. They burst out laughing. I laughed along with them, then asked what the sign meant. That made them laugh even harder. I then walked back to my car and returned with my camera, which really put them in hysterics. I took several pictures of the moose and donkey as two of the kids rolled on the ground howling. I never did go in the bar, figuring I'd done my civic duty by spending ten minutes playing the village idiot.

But at least I had pictures to prove my story. Who knows? Maybe Boomer would want to buy them from me and have them enlarged into a poster for his living room. That would impress the ladies.

As I drove back toward the U.S. border, I began to think Canadians should be awarded some kind of Nobel Prize for outlandish signs. But no sooner had I crossed back into New

Hampshire than I came upon a logging truck with New Hampshire license plates and noticed the truck had an important message painted in large glitter letters on its side. The message simply said "Doin' it Doggie Style." And I thought the state motto was "Live Free or Die."

After my Canadian adventure, I fished a portion of the Connecticut River, then drove eastward toward Maine. The temperature had dropped considerably and forecasters were calling for rain, so I scrapped my plans to camp. Using my visitors' guide, I found the cheapest lodging possible. It was a bed-and-breakfast that sounded like it had all the comforts of home. The B&B was in an old farmhouse run by a friendly but eccentric older woman. That evening we chatted in her kitchen by the comfort of her old Glenwood stove, since it had become quite cold out. She told me how most of her family had moved out of the area to find work elsewhere, and since she had this big old house all to herself she opened it up as a B&B a few years earlier to help with expenses. She gave me the history of the house but failed to tell me that my room had no heat. I figured that out at about one o'clock in the morning, as I lay shivering in my bed with just the single blanket covering me. There were no extra blankets in the closet, so I finally opened the bedroom door in hopes that any heat from the rest of the house would enter my room. Big mistake. Four cats came rushing in, hopping on the bureau, the bed, and eventually ending up under the bed, where they brawled, meowed, and did whatever cats do in the middle of the night.

I was worried that the next visitor to my room might be the eccentric woman. (Read Stephen King's *Misery* to see what happens between young male writers and crazy women.) The cats had to go, so under the bed I went and the cats ran out the other side. I was able to grab one and fling it out the door, and the others followed. Shutting the door, my shivering resumed, and I realized this was a lose-lose situation. An open door meant cats running berserk in my room; a closed door meant a cold, equally sleepless night. These options reminded me of the old childhood question: Would you rather die of heat in the desert, or cold in the Arctic? The situation was getting dire, when I remembered my down sleeping bag in the car. I tiptoed out of my room, kicked a cat (accidentally, of course), and retrieved my sleeping bag. I returned to my room, shut the door, and crawled into the cold and clammy bag. Snuggling down toward the bottom of the bag, my body heat gradually started to warm it up, and I congratulated myself on my resourcefulness. Then something pounced on me.

My arms were pinned inside the bag—reminiscent of my night sleeping on the dock—useless to fend off the creature that was attacking. The creature moved from my midsection up toward my head, and I thought it might be moving in for the kill. Then it licked my ear. A cat!

I survived the night and realized it could have been worse. Suppose it had been the crazy lady who had licked my ear? Suppose I had liked it?

The following day, without much sleep, I headed into Maine, and for the first time in my life was stopped by a game warden while fishing. I never even heard him come up behind me; he just appeared and asked if I was having a good day and, oh, could he see my license. Thank God I had remembered to buy a license that morning. While he was checking it out, I asked where the fish were biting and he responded, "In the river." But at least he said it with a smile.

"Guess that was a stupid question," I said.

"Not really, I've heard a lot worse."

"Like what?"

"One out-of-stater asked me how old a deer has to be before it turns into a moose."

"Wow, that is bad."

"Another one wanted to know if it was going to be a bad winter because he saw a squirrel bury a peanut."

"Any others?"

"None off the top of my head, just the usual excuses for poaching. But you can call headquarters and they can tell you a few more."

I did just that and here is a sampling:

"Is the public allowed to fish at the state fish hatcheries?"

"How many lobsters does it take to make Lobster Newburg for forty people?"

"I have a four-month-old daughter; does she have to wear a lifejacket in our boat?"

"I called to report I was stung by a bee while moving brush."

"Do I need to take a safety course to get a fishing license?"

"How do I get rid of all the white phlegm around my house left by snakes?"

"Do you have any confiscated monkeys you want to give away?"

"I'm thinking of purchasing a submarine; what regulations apply?"

Later as I pushed on to Moosehead Lake, I wished I had talked to the warden a little longer; maybe we would have discussed the moose population in Maine, and I might have learned a thing or two to keep me out of trouble.

I had driven up the eastern side of Moosehead Lake hoping to get one of those "perfect" wildlife shots, when I saw a moose feeding across a marsh and decided this was my chance. Launching my canoe into the water, I was pleasantly surprised to see that the wind would blow the canoe toward the moose, allowing me to work the camera and not worry too much about paddling. Trying to get a great wildlife photo takes patience, so I took my time, letting the breeze work me closer. As I watched the moose through the camera's viewfinder, it seemed like I was watching a nature movie, and I relaxed and enjoyed the show.

As I got closer to the moose, I realized it was a big bull, feeding contentedly, with aquatic plants streaming out of its mouth. I found it hard to believe that something this big still lives in the wild. The moose must have known I was approaching, yet beyond a casual glance my way, it made no move to retreat to the forest.

Onward I came, fiddling with my zoom lens and snapping a picture every sixty seconds. Soon, the head of the moose was filling the frame of my camera, and the notion came to me that maybe I was closer than I realized. I looked over the top of the camera, and my heart skipped a beat. The moose was no more than twenty feet away. The moose realized the same thing, deciding he didn't particularly like being my model, and didn't particularly like me interrupting his meal. He let me know by glaring at me. I was close enough to see a little patch of fur-covered skin below his chin swing ever so slowly. I could even see the flies buzzing around his head. The flies were not a good sign, because they were probably pissing the moose off, and now he had an intruder to contend with.

I should have avoided making eye contact with him, but I was too scared not to; I didn't dare move a muscle. Moose can grow to be seven feet high at the shoulder and weigh twelve hundred pounds. He looked every bit that big. I prayed he would submerge his head under the water for another mouthful of plants, which would give me the chance to grab the paddle and get the hell out of there. But he didn't take his eyes off me, as if incredulous that something would have the audacity to come directly toward him.

The moose broke the tension when he decided he had had enough. He lowered his head, let out a deep grunt, and then took a step toward me. I must have looked like an animated cartoon the way I back paddled for all I was worth. The canoe almost capsized, and that would have meant curtains, but the God of Dumb Outdoorsmen was with me, and I put distance between the moose and me.

I recall reading how Thoreau described a moose as "a great frightened rabbit, with their long ears and half-inquisitive, half-frightened looks: the true denizens of the forest." Had Thoreau been in my canoe he never would have described the moose as a great frightened rabbit. He might, however, have used that description for me.

I'm not alone with my aggressive moose story; bulls can be ornery anytime of year, especially during the fall rut, when they have the single-minded purpose of mating. (Kinda sounds like Boomer, only he's the year-round type.) I met a hunter in Greenville, Maine, after my moose scare, and when he stopped laughing about my tale, he confided that his brother Al had an even closer call while out deer hunting.

> Al was moving along the edge of a swamp when he startled a big bull moose. The moose immediately charged, and my brother was so surprised he dropped his gun and ran. He turned and looked back and the moose was just fifteen or twenty feet away, so he ducked behind a sapling. The moose rammed the tree with its antlers, and Al thought it was going to be lights out. Apparently this happened repeatedly, and Al had to keep pivoting around a small maple, keeping it between him and the moose. He tried shouting and waving his arms, but nothing would scare this bull away. Finally he just prayed the tree would stand up to the beating. Eventually the moose tired and walked away.

Since that time I keep track of the moose stories I hear, and trust me, there's been plenty. One schoolteacher I met described how, while on a sight-seeing drive in Maine with a friend, they spotted a bull moose with a huge rack of antlers standing in the road a short distance away. Wanting to get a picture, they inched her small Toyota closer. The moose wheeled around and suddenly charged the car, pushing it back ten feet. Not satisfied, the moose then started to climb on the Toyota, and the women slid down into the foot well, thinking the moose's hooves were going to come through the windshield. The moose then moved to the side of the car and rammed it one more time for good measure before sauntering down the road as if nothing had happened.

Another report from Maine described how a bull that had been rejected by a cow took out his frustration on the nearest object, a house. He rammed the house, tearing out the siding and smashing the windows with his antlers. Then he turned his attention on the car parked in the driveway and inflicted $7,000 worth of damage.

Moose are not to be trifled with. Supreme Court Justice William O. Douglas was an avid outdoorsman, and in his book *East to Katahdin* he refers to the strength of the moose when recalling a story his Maine guide told him. "The old Guide," wrote Douglas, "was witness to a fight between a bear and a moose, an event the moose won by breaking the bear's back with his forefeet." So for those of us who might be concerned about black bears, remember it's the moose who's king of the forest.

Moose aren't the only animals that do unpredictable things. Even deer will surprise you—just ask the lady at a golf course in Massachusetts who recently had the misfortune to be standing in the way of a running deer. The *Boston Herald* reported, "An Ashburnham woman practicing her putting was injured when a deer that tried to use her as a hurdle failed to clear her head." Local fire captain Ricci Bushioni explained, "When the deer jumped, it hit her in the mouth and I guess it knocked some of her teeth out." And you thought you had bad days on the golf course.

I stayed the night in Greenville and had a great night's sleep at an inn without cats or cobwebs. I still had three days of vacation left, with the final night and day to be spent with Cogs back at the cabin. Before I left Maine I hiked Mount Kineo, which rises like the Rock of Gibraltar from a peninsula near the middle of Moosehead Lake. It was one of the best hikes I've ever had, with a different view appearing after each successive fifteen minutes of climbing of the mountain. Thoreau also hiked Kineo and had a similar feeling for the mountain, writing with verve about the great vistas: "The clouds breaking away a little, we had a glorious wild view, as we ascended, of the broad lake with its fluctuating surface and numerous forest-clad islands."

From Kineo it was one long ride back to the cabin, first wending my way south on Route 201 along the Kennebec River and then west on Route 2, which took me through western Maine, northern New Hampshire, and back into Vermont's Northeast Kingdom.

Once at the cabin, I made a fire outside, cracked open a beer, and waited for the arrival of Cogs, who was coming to the cabin directly from a business meeting he had in Vermont. I had spent so many days alone I could hardly wait for his appearance. But since I hadn't spoken with Cogs in a week, I figured there was a good chance he might not even show.

When Cogs did not arrive by 10:30 P.M., I doused the fire with water and spread a blanket in the clearing in front of the cabin to view the stars before bed. Without any light pollution the stars were crystal clear, and I watched the slow path of a satellite move across the night sky. I'd gotten over the fear that a bear might stumble upon me, and it didn't bother me to lie alone in the woods in the black night . . . until Cogs arrived and planted a new concern.

I could hear his car toiling up the hill, and in the night's still-ness it sounded like a Mack truck. I moved my blanket to the edge of the clearing so he wouldn't run me over, and then Cogs pulled up in front of the cabin, parked, and got out. He faced the cabin and in a singsong voice yodeled, "Oh, Toouuuggg, your special guest is here." The last thing Cogs expected was the growling noise I made from the other side of the clearing, and he spun around and crouched behind his car. Then I turned, aimed the flashlight directly at his head, and zapped him with the light.

"I sure hope that's you, Mikey. And if it's not, I surrender."

"Well, Pilgrim," I said in my best John Wayne voice, "just leave your wallet on the steps, saddle up, and get back to town."

"Very funny, Toug." Cogs slowly made his way through the darkness toward me and my flashlight.

"Isn't it a little late to be having a picnic?" he asked when he could see me lying on the blanket.

"Just doin' a little stargazing. Grab your coat and get a beer from the fridge and join me."

Cogs returned with a couple of beers, and we sat and talked about his life in the flatlands and my North Country vacation, lying on our backs looking up at the heavens.

"Toug," Cogs said, "You get more vacation time than anyone I know."

"That's true, but I don't take any time in the winter and save it all for the summer. I've still got eight days left even after this trip."

"What are you going to do with it all?"

"Probably come back up here."

"You need to branch out, boy, see new horizons, get yourself . . ."

"Wow," I suddenly said, "did you see that shooting star? It looked like it was so close I could touch it!"

"It was a firefly, you idiot."

"Oh."

"Did you know," said Cogs, getting serious, "that the Milky Way is so bright because there are so many stars in it, and that the galaxy we are looking at is just one of many?"

"Can you believe this goes on forever?" I said, meaning space.

"Well, actually it doesn't. Now they say there's an end to it."

"So what's after the end?"

"They don't really say."

"Then I say it goes on forever."

"But nothing can go on forever."

"But it can't just end; there has to be something after that, even if its nothingness."

"What the hell is 'nothingness'? That's not even a word."

"I don't know, I think space is beyond the realm of the human mind to grasp. Only a higher life form could comprehend it."

"Well," said Cogs in a knowing tone, "if you want to read about higher life forms, read Whitley Strieber's books. But don't read 'em up here."

"Why not?"

"Just don't; they're terrifying—they open your mind to things you never even considered."

"Why is it worse to read him at the cabin?"

"Do you ever want to come up here alone again?"

"Of course, I love it."

"Well, don't read his books, 'cause one is about a guy alone at his cabin in the Adirondacks who gets visited by aliens."

"Maybe I won't read it anywhere."

"And the aliens take this guy and study him, probing him everywhere and they don't care that he's in pain."

"They don't?"

"No, they view him the way you would a worm."

Needless to say, I never read the book about the cabin in the Adirondacks; I wasn't going to tempt fate.

My entry in the guest book summarized my trip through the North Country, but ended with the final night's thoughts:

*I ask you, did Daniel Boone, John Colter, or Thoreau have to contend with alien abductions? I was just getting comfortable in the woods until Cogs showed up . . .*

Cogs's entry had a different note of concern:

*I'm worried about Mike. I found him lying in the dark, growling at the moon. Diagnosis: woods queer. Remedy: sell the cabin, buy a condo on Miami Beach, and start wearing gold chains to go with your inflatable polyester pants.*

# CHAPTER 13

# BULLS, BOOMER, AND TREE CUTTING MADE DIFFICULT

*In nature there are neither rewards nor punishments—
there are consequences.*

—R. G. INGERSOLL

The cabin would be nothing without friends. As much as I began to enjoy coming up alone, the trips with friends were equally special. During the fall of the fifth year, Boomer joined me for the first four days of a weeklong vacation where we spent part of the time at the cabin and the other part exploring northern Vermont.

We started the week with an early morning float trip down the Lamoille River in my canoe, which allowed us to reach some stretches of water that few anglers had fished. We took turns being in the stern, guiding the canoe, while the other fished from the bow. Oftentimes the one in the bow merely had to let his fly float downriver ahead of the canoe and a fish would rise, sip it in, and then skip across the water when we set the hook. As we approached the best-looking pools, we would beach the canoe, then slowly advance by wading to improve the accuracy of our limited casting abilities. It was one of the best days of fishing we'd had in some time, catching rainbow trout from eight to thirteen inches. But that's not what Boomer will remember about the trip.

Near the end of our outing we floated through a dairy farm, and Boomer suddenly stopped paddling.

"Will you look at that?" he whispered.

I glanced downstream to see a bull humping a cow just two feet from the river. "Geez," I said, "I've never seen that before."

"Look how big it is!" Boomer exclaimed, and he wasn't talking about the bull's body.

The bull heard us and turned its head toward the oncoming canoe. He was still going at it, but he was staring at us. I could see the whites of his eyes and it made me uncomfortable.

"I think he wants a little privacy."

Boomer shook his head. "No way, I've gotta get a better look at this."

"I don't think that's a good idea. The current is sweeping us toward the bank the bull's on."

"Nothing's going to happen. Be a man, we're gonna glide right by."

When two men are in a canoe with one paddling forward and the other one back paddling, you might think the canoe would stay stationary. On a river, however, the current wins, and we went downstream, getting closer and closer to the action.

When we were within fifteen feet, Boomer finally showed concern. "God, we're dead if he decides to charge." Then he added, "I think we have a new winner of the Longest Dong Award."

We had both stopped paddling, and as we glided closer, neither of us moved a muscle. The bull gave us a stare that seemed to say, "If I see so much as one smirk, I'll rub you out."

When we were safely past, Boomer didn't even bother to fish anymore. "That was unbelievable. All the times I've been to Vermont, I've never seen anything like that. Now I know there's truth to the expression 'hung like a bull.'"

I laughed along with him, more out of relief than in response to Boomer's revelation. This was one of the few times Boomer got me into a vulnerable situation where I emerged without a scratch.

The real trouble started an hour later when we were done fishing and heading toward Stowe, Vermont. Along the way we stopped at a restaurant we'd never been to before. The food was good and the price was right, but our waitress, who we'll call Gladys, had a problem: She broke wind repeatedly. She did it in a relatively quiet, sneaky sort of way, and she probably thought she was fooling everyone in the place. To cover the noise of the fart, she'd cough, then ease the deadly, noxious gas into space as she moved from table to table, refreshing people's coffee. By the time the odor hit the nearest victims, Gladys figured she was safely out of blame.

Her little ruse worked the first time, when Boomer looked at me and said, "You're disgusting. I'm trying to enjoy my coffee and you do that in a public eatery."

There was little defense I could offer, but when the deadly fumes hit again, I began to put two and two together, noticing the air was fouled only when Gladys was in the dining area, and only when she was on the move. I'm sure I even heard a little squeak from her direction before one cloud came over. *Oh, the smell!*

Again, Boomer blamed me, this time quipping, "What have I done to deserve this? In God's name, I beg you to cease and desist. The eggs will be here any minute."

I figured similar conversations were going on at other tables, with one person blaming the other.

"Boomer," I whispered, "I think it's Gladys."

"Don't blame the waitress for your problem. I smelled it earlier in the canoe."

"That was the cow patties where the bull was."

"I'm not buying it."

"I can prove it," I said. "The next time the waitress comes over, simply count to three after she leaves and see if the smell hits again."

When it happened just as I predicted, I felt exonerated and we giggled like schoolgirls.

Then Gladys came over and with a not-so-friendly tone of voice asked us to keep it down.

"Folks are trying to enjoy breakfast," she said.

*Enjoy breakfast!* I almost screamed, the nerve of her telling us we were ruining someone's meal. But she was a lot bigger than me and I wasn't about to argue, so I simply nodded.

Boomer glanced at me and said, "How do I know it still wasn't you? You could have been holding it in, waiting for the waitress to appear and then letting it go three seconds after she left."

Just then something caught our attention. The cook stopped flipping the bacon and picked up her whining baby and placed it on the counter. Then she proceeded to change its diapers.

I kicked Boomer under the table and whispered, "I rest my case. Enjoy your eggs."

After breakfast we headed west toward Stowe, planning our two-day outing as we went. We were in my car with the canoe strapped to the roof. I made sure I secured the straps, remembering all too well the canoe's space launch the last time Boomer had tied it to the top.

"I don't want to camp out," announced Boomer.

"But Stowe costs a fortune," I replied. "Besides, I thought we were going to hike Mount Mansfield. And you went out of your way to borrow a down sleeping bag for me and pack your tent."

"Look, I'll make a deal with you. I'll hike Mount Mansfield this afternoon if we get a cheap motel room tonight. Then we can camp out the next night and you can do your nature thing."

"But why not camp out both nights?" I asked.

"No offense, but staying at the cabin is like camping out. When are we gonna put running water in that place?"

"Probably never. I want to buy a home outside of Boston, so I'm saving my money."

"Why not sell the cabin and use that money for the down payment?"

"I think I'd regret it. I've heard a couple of my dad's friends say they used to have places on lakes that they sold and now they kick themselves."

"But a home in the Boston area is a better investment."

Boomer was right, of course, but I was in the old proverbial mode of wanting my cake and eating it too. "I want both," I said, "it's just that Massachusetts is so damn expensive."

"I've got a solution. You have six acres at the cabin. Sell two or three, and that should give you enough money to help with the down payment on a home."

We drove in silence while I considered that option. It wasn't a bad idea.

Boomer enjoyed his newfound pragmatism and expounded upon his plan. "It's win-win. You get to keep the cabin and still have pond frontage yet get a decent home outside of Boston. You don't want to have to settle for a condo, 'cause you'd be miserable there."

Boomer did seem to have all the answers, and he was right about me and condos.

"Well, I'll think about it. I think I'd do it if I could get $10,000 for three acres. That's all I'd need for a home with a manageable mortgage."

"Glad I could be of service," said Boomer.

"What about you? You should be saving for a house. A guy at work our age bought one last year and he's already made $20,000."

"I can't see myself in suburbia. I'd feel weird around all those married couples. I hate to mow the grass and that stuff. It's different for you—you like to putter around. You've been growing gardens since the sixth grade, so you'd feel right at home."

Boomer was making perfect sense and it was scary. *Maybe,* I thought, *I should let him call the shots on this trip and just let things flow.* After all, he went along with most of my plans on past weekends.

We drove west on Route 15, following the Lamoille River as it gathered strength on its journey to Lake Champlain. We planned the rest of our two-day outing, agreeing to make a big loop of northwestern Vermont, fishing wherever the opportunity presented itself, and ending up back at the cabin.

"It's about time we're branching out from the cabin," said Boomer. "We might actually meet some girls tonight."

"We may even meet some when we get back to the cabin," I said. "That fiddlers' contest I've been telling you about gets a good crowd."

I had no idea if the fiddlers' contest that was to be held near the cabin attracted more than a dozen people, but I really wanted to go and I didn't want to go alone.

"Fiddling," said Boomer, "is one step up from hog calling. I doubt the women there will be the kind I had in mind. Stowe will be where the ladies are. But the way you're driving, we'll never get there."

I was driving a tad slow, looking out toward the river, pondering new sections to fish.

"I'm surprised you don't drive with just one finger on the top of the steering wheel, or at the very least, just one hand. Then when your fellow motorists pass by, you can do a little country wave by raising a finger or two from the wheel. And I've got to get you one of those hats the farmers wear—might impress the father-in-law-to-be at the big farm, I mean the 'pig farm.'"

Boomer was immensely satisfied with his attempt at sarcasm and wouldn't let it drop. Reaching for the radio dial, he said, "Let's see if we can find a little Glenn Miller."

We did eventually reach Stowe, securing lodging at the cheapest place we could find, a boardinghouse with Spartan, bunk-bed-lined rooms and a single bathroom shared by all guests. Then we drove up toward Mount Mansfield via Smugglers Notch. Boomer said he had already hiked Mansfield years ago, so we changed our plans and hiked the Long Trail to Sterling Pond and Madonna Peak. It was a great hike through a landscape of stunted spruce, fir, and rare Arctic plants, with Sterling Pond resting in majestic isolation.

Boomer enjoyed the hike, so the least I could do was to repay the favor, and that night we went out and had a grand old time. I recall getting up onstage at one of the dancing establishments and playing the drums until the bouncers carried me outside. Boomer, true friend that he is, sneaked me back inside through a door that led into the kitchen area. Then we casually made our way back to the lounge, where we danced the night away. (Yes, we really found girls who would dance with us.)

Later, when we got back to the boardinghouse, I was terribly hungry and went wandering to see what I could rustle up. There was a community refrigerator for all the guests to use, and in the freezer was a carton of chocolate ice cream. The temptation was just too great. I'm a chocolate nut, and I decided I needed this ice cream more than its true owner ever could. I ate almost the whole half-gallon but couldn't finish the last couple of bites, so I carried the carton back to our room to get rid of the evidence.

The next morning after showering I was walking back to my room when I heard loud voices coming from the kitchen area.

"I don't know what you're talking about." It was Boomer's voice, loud and defiant.

"You stole my ice cream and you're going to get me a new one."

This second voice was tense with anger. I understood what they were talking about and decided to ease back into an alcove and stay out of view. The next voice I heard was Boomer's.

"I repeat, I did not eat your ice cream, and I'd like you to get out of my face."

"Listen, wise guy, the trail of melted ice cream leads right to your door."

Things were heating up. The right thing to do was for me to walk out and explain what really happened. Instead I slid farther back out of sight. This was a priceless moment and I didn't want to interrupt.

"For the last time," Boomer said, "I don't know what you're talking about, and I don't need to listen to some jerk like you."

Boomer stomped off to our room and slammed the door. I peeked out, but the ice cream man had followed him and I pulled my head back. The ice cream man just stood at our door for a couple of seconds, obviously thinking things over, and then stormed off.

I made a dash to our room. Boomer was packing when he looked up at me.

"Some asshole just accused me of eating his ice cream. We almost got in a fistfight."

"Yeah, I heard the last part of it. You held your ground. Let's just get out of here so there's no trouble."

I had started throwing things into my overnight bag when I noticed the empty ice cream container beneath my pants. I glanced toward Boomer, who was still busy packing, then quickly put the container in my bag.

The first time Boomer will understand what really happened will be when he reads this.

From Stowe, we pushed northwestward past Burlington, cross-ing a portion of Lake Champlain on the bridge that leads to South Hero and Grand Isle. We had heard about the great small-mouth bass fishing in the lake, and we had high hopes of catch-ing a trophy-size bass. The countryside was quite different than the mountains around the cabin. Here was gentle rolling ter-rain, much of it open fields leading down to the sparkling waters of Lake Champlain, where a few handsome homes had total privacy. One small, rustic home on Grand Isle commanded a far-reaching vista of the lake, with a beach not far from the road. It was such a pleasant spot we pulled over and walked down to the beach, where I could take some pictures. The home owner must have wondered what we were doing, because he came out of the house, walked over to us, and said, "May I help you?"

Boomer responded in a way that showed he had slept through English class the day Miss Eaton worked on little-known verbs. He turned to the home owner and said, "Your place appalls me."

The home owner looked like he'd been punched. "What?"

"I said your place appalls me. We were driving by and we just had to stop."

"Get the hell off my property you insulting jerk."

Now it was Boomer's turn to look like he'd been punched.

I tried to help, saying, "What he means is that—"

The home owner cut me off and, like an enraged bull, made a menacing move toward us. "Get out!"

Back in the car, I screamed at Boomer, "Why did you say that?"

"Because I liked his beach and home."

Then it hit me that Boomer didn't know what the word "appall" meant. Maybe he was thinking of "appeal," or maybe he had gone through life complimenting people by saying they appalled him. That would explain his recent dry spell with women.

We continued north through the islands of Lake Champlain, stopping once to launch the canoe and go fishing. We hadn't bargained for waves that made us feel like we were on the ocean, and neither of us wanted to tempt fate by staying out long. Boomer uncharacteristically suggested we head in and get off the water. Maybe he was spooked by the two strange encounters he'd had in the last twenty-four hours: the enraged ice cream man and the insulted home owner both threatened him with bodily harm.

But I'm glad I got Boomer in trouble, because for the rest of the trip the tables were turned. We camped out the next night at North Hero State Park, and the temperature dropped while a steady rain fell. Inside our tent we were dry, but for some inexplicable reason I was freezing despite having Boomer's borrowed down sleeping bag. Boomer snored away while I curled into a ball. My extremities were especially cold, so I dug through my overnight bag and pulled out underwear and undershirts, because all my socks were wet from fishing. I wrapped the undershirts around my toes and put two pairs of underwear on my head, reckoning that most body heat is lost through the top of the head.

Still I froze. I swore that if I survived I'd quit being cheap and purchase the best sleeping bag that money could buy, the kind climbers use on Mount Everest, or at least one that could handle thirty-degree fall nights. After an hour of shivering I got out my flashlight, located the tag on the sleeping bag, and read these words: "Made from 100% polyester." I thought I'd lose my mind. I was going to wake Boomer up, but I knew that wouldn't help me get to sleep. I put on my coat and got back into the sleeping bag and mercifully fell asleep.

When I awoke, Boomer was sitting up in the tent as if waiting for me to rise. Then he shook his head and spoke.

"Do you always sleep with your underwear on your head?"

As mad as I was at Boomer, I think I was angrier at the weather forecasters. Before we left home, the TV weather forecasters had called for the next four days to be warm and sunny throughout New England. I should have known better. They are pretty good at predicting the next day's weather (which should be easy enough since all they really have to do is call Chicago, find out what it's doing there, and it's a good bet the prevailing winds will bring that weather here in twenty-four hours). But how these weather guys can look, with a straight face, into the camera and say it's going to be such-and-such in four days is beyond me. They seem to be wrong 50 percent of the time, so anyone could flip a coin between sun and clouds and do the same. Worst of all, many of them act like they have a role in the weather, saying such inane things as "We're going to bring you some sunny days," or "We're working on getting rid of those nasty clouds."

Had I known it was going to rain, I might have listened to Boomer and gotten a room both nights. I'd rather have my wisdom teeth pulled or be trapped with an insurance salesman than be stuck in a tent while it's raining. One author I've read described rain in the forest as "soothing." Maybe a brief shower might evoke that feeling, but anything more turns the calming effect into gloom, which in turn can become depressing if the rain carries on for a couple of days. After a few hours of rain, the dampness lays its clammy grip on you and you feel like a mushroom may sprout under your armpit. That's why magazine ads for camping trips always show two smiling people standing by their tent in brilliant sunshine. A more realistic portrayal would be a sagging tent with two disheveled campers swatting flies while they struggle to get a campfire started in damp conditions. And for real authenticity they should have people with stubble or dirt on their faces and matted, greasy, tangled hair. Better yet, show those same two people arguing, or perhaps have one sulking in the tent while the other huddles by a miserable little campfire with a hot dog on a stick.

As we packed the tent, Boomer poured salt in the wound. "Why is it," he asked, "that every time I camp with you it rains?"

We drove off the islands at East Alburg and through the Missisquoi National Wildlife Refuge, a huge shallow-water marsh delta that looked especially dreary in the foggy mist.

Because of the rain, we abandoned our plan to fish and take the scenic back roads on our return trip to the cabin, and instead drove down Interstate 89 all the way to Montpelier.

The rain had stopped and streaks of sunshine broke through the western skies. I tried to cheer Boomer up, as he said little during the long drive down from the islands. "Well, the weather should be great for tomorrow's fiddlers' contest. Why don't we pick up a few groceries and I'll make a great dinner when we get to the cabin."

"Sounds good. Just don't buy that iceberg lettuce. Spread your wings a little and at least buy some lettuce that has a taste and is green instead of white."

"Any other instructions?"

"Yeah, don't buy those packaged lunch meats—go to the deli counter."

"Should I be taking notes?"

"Please do. Remember to buy the little red potatoes, not those big boring lumpy ones. And let's get a nice tenderloin instead of hamburg."

"Are you done?"

"Just one more thing. If you make the sandwiches tomorrow, don't let the mustard touch the bread. Spread it on the meat, please."

I was beginning to feel like we were married, and we'd only been together for four days.

The next day, we arrived at the fiddlers' contest in the late afternoon, bringing a large blanket to lie on and enjoy the music. Boomer may have been a little disappointed that it was just a local gathering with a couple of food vendors and folks sitting around in lawn chairs, but he seemed to enjoy the music as much as I did. It's not every day you hear fiddle music in New England.

Everything was going fine until a rusted old station wagon pulled up and out came four grubby men and four women who obviously had been living in the hills a bit too long. They might have been husbands and wives, brothers and sisters, or both.

One of the men had a beard with no mustache, and Boomer stared at him as if he had just emerged from a UFO. I can't say that I'd ever seen such an odd beard, but I tried not to stare, although I did notice that in addition to his upper lip being clean-shaven, the area just under his lower lip was also hair-free, making the beard look like a thin helmet strap.

Now the name "Boomer" might lead you to believe he's a good old boy like the ones in the station wagon, but Boomer, being somewhat of a preppie, is more at home with the deck-shoed boating crowd at Newport, Rhode Island, or Essex, Connecticut, than up here in the hills. The sight of these modern-day hillbillies was a new experience for him, and he couldn't help but gawk.

But he should have. People, especially men with half-beards, don't like to be gawked at. Our bearded friend walked right over to Boomer, and I thought for sure he was going to punch his lights out. Instead he said, "You're not from around here, are you?"

Boomer recovered and explained he was just up for a long weekend and loved fiddle music, although I doubt he knew a fiddle from a ukulele. Somehow the two of them actually hit it off, and they walked over to the other hillbillies, where Boomer was introduced as if he were a celebrity. I tagged along and got a few halfhearted hellos, wondering why they took a shine to Boomer and not me. Then it hit me: I must have looked like one of them, with my dirty, powder blue polyester pants, old winged-collar shirt open at the neck, three-day stubble, and hair matted down by my fishing hat. Boomer, on the other hand, had on tan Docker slacks, a polo shirt, and a clean white sweater draped over one shoulder.

One of the female hillbillies (I believe they're called "hillbilli-ettes") went back to the station wagon and returned with a cooler full of Rolling Rock beer. The fiddlers seemed to know the hillbillies, and they started to play with a renewed enthusiasm. With dusk falling, Boomer started partying with his friends.

An hour later, Boomer's slacks were covered in grass stains and his sweater smudged with a large dirt spot, the result of trying to dance to fiddle music, which is next to impossible. No one tried anything remotely similar to a square dance, but instead did a kind of jig, with Boomer leading the way. Each time a song ended they all clapped wildly, a bit too loudly. I eased away from the group, back to where the older folks were sitting in lawn chairs, and struck up a conversation with a couple of eighty-year-old gents, one of whom kept taking his false teeth out and putting them back in.

Twenty-some odd songs later, Boomer was still going strong, only now he was slow dancing (no, not with old Half-beard), even though the fiddlers were still playing fast tunes. Boomer's hands were all over his dance partner, who was the same lady who got the beer cooler from the station wagon. She had to be twice Boomer's age.

One of the hillbillies, who was leaning against the barn and smoking, was paying special attention to Boomer and his lady friend.

I didn't like the looks of things, and after a couple more songs I interrupted Boomer and his new girlfriend, telling him we best be getting back to the cabin.

Boomer thought that was a swell idea. He hollered over to Half-beard, "You all want to come up to our cabin? I think we've got a little Jack Daniels!"

I was mortified. I did not want these people at my cabin under any circumstances, but especially not at night, and not after drinking. Too late.

Half-beard nodded, smiling. He rounded up his troops and they piled into the station wagon.

The girl was still in Boomer's arms. "You can ride with us," he said.

"No, she can't," I snapped.

The girl didn't move. But Boomer saw my face, illuminated by the station wagon's headlights. He gave her a quick kiss and said, "You ride with them and I'll see you at the cabin. Maybe we can go for a moonlight swim."

When Boomer and I got in my car, I calmly shut the door, then screamed, "You idiot! They're all shit-faced and there's no way they're going to my cabin. I don't even want them to know what town it's in!"

"What's your problem? The guy with the beard is really funny and the girl is sweet."

"Jesus, Boomer, have you taken a close look at her? Sweet is not the word I'd use. Besides, I think she's with one of the other guys."

"You mean the one who was leaning up against the barn?"

"So you noticed. He looked like he was going to kill you."

"He did, didn't he?" Boomer paused, appearing to gather his wits. "Now what?"

Our new friends pulled up beside my car and honked their horn.

We pulled out of the parking lot, and then I floored it, flying over the dirt roads. When I saw a driveway to a trailer home ahead, I swerved in and killed the headlights. Two minutes later the station wagon went rumbling by.

For once Boomer didn't even argue.

Boomer headed back to Boston the next day, and it was so quiet at the cabin I felt a little disconcerted. To ward off the encroaching loneliness, I threw myself into the fine art of puttering. I define puttering as tasks that seem more like fun than work, and the outcome doesn't have to be perfect. Over the last year I had actually learned the difference between a regular screwdriver and a Phillips-head, and felt smug that I knew what "plumb" meant. Yes, I was a true putterer. (Helen and Scott Nearing, authors of *Living the Good Life,* expressed similar sentiments: "After all is said and done, it is foolish and wasteful to let professional building tradesmen think out, plan, construct and at the end of the job thrill with the joy of work well done.")

Of course, I should add that the puttering I was going to undertake was minor stuff, not like the guy who rents a backhoe, strikes a gas line, and blows his house up. I also made it a rule to avoid tinkering with anything electrical, which is well beyond my limited know-how. But minor jobs at the cabin were all mine, and I figured if I didn't like the way they turned out, I'd recruit Cogs and Boomer to fix them.

On the first day after Boomer left, I made a coatrack (constructed from a beech tree, using the sawed-off limbs as the hooks) and a bench that I placed at the halfway point on the trail down to the pond. Between each project I'd sit on the porch and have a cold drink, finding that the mix of rest, recreation, and puttering was about the most relaxing and satisfying way to spend a day I could imagine.

In the corporate world I would be popping aspirin by 2:00 P.M. for eyestrain, and the muscles in my neck and shoulders would be as taut as steel springs. I'm convinced those were the manifestations of being forced to work as fast as you can with no real physical activity. The sheer pressure of rushing could make anyone develop symptoms of stress. But if you're allowed to do the best job you can, in a reasonable amount of time, I'm convinced we could all work ten-hour days and be energized by what we accomplish, rather than demoralized by more tasks waiting in the wings.

The next day I finally tackled the job of painting the cabin, embarrassed to say I had let four years go by with little or no paint on the exterior. I chose a barn red color and white trim, and I laid on the paint with the zeal of an artist who has been denied the brush. When I had painted as high as I could reach, I built a ladder out of two-by-fours that worked fine except for the very peak of the A-frame, where only an extension ladder would reach.

I enjoyed this pattern of puttering by day and reading my mountain-man/outdoor books by night. I'd been up at the cabin alone enough over the last few years to realize that extended solitude could become unhealthy, referred to by a friend from northern Maine as "woods queer." When he first used that expression, I asked him what he meant and he simply said, "I've seen it happen to my own brother; he lived alone in the backwoods, never seeing another soul. When I visited him, he acted odd, almost paranoid of my presence. He'd been in the woods too long." Well, I didn't want to be woods queer, especially since I still had to go back to an apartment outside Boston shared with four other guys, put on a suit and tie each morning, and ride the train to the city for my job. You simply can't do those things if you're woods queer.

On the third morning sans Boomer, I combated isolation by driving fifty miles round-trip for breakfast, then worked at the cabin until noon, followed by a quarter-mile walk to my nearest neighbor, Millie, for a chat. Millie did most of the chatting. On good days she would talk about the wildlife she had seen, such as mallards, a fawn, and a fisher. And she always asked me if I'd seen Herb the bear, which I had not since the day in the logging field. When she was in one of her moods, she'd talk about her "damn kids" trying to put her away in a rest home and how she'd never see her cottage again. You would think living here was heaven, but when Millie mentioned her granddaughter in college, she surprised me by saying, "I told her that when she graduates she better not move back up here, or I'll kick her butt all the way to China."

"But you love it here."

"This is no place for someone just starting out. There's nothing here for them. If she comes back here, she'll fall into a rut, have a kid within a year and be divorced within three, and have a piss-poor job to boot."

I told Millie how ironic it was, her telling her granddaughter to never come back, when half the people I know down in suburbia dream of one day moving to the country. I also said there's another way to look at lower-paying jobs up here. "The people down in the cities work like dogs to be able to afford a second home up here so that they can rush up on a Friday and rush back on a Sunday. But if a person loves these mountains, they might be better off taking whatever job they can get up here, 'cause at least they're where they want to be."

"I don't care about all that," she said, "I just want her to get a start somewhere else. Then later, if she thinks this is what she wants, she can come back. 'Course, by that time I'll be long gone and my son will have sold the cottage."

I excused myself, walked back up the hill, and finished my puttering. For dinner I had gotten into the habit of using a gas grill I'd bought, and if I do say so, I turned out some pretty decent meals. Some nights I'd prepare a couple of trout I had caught, baking them on the grill with onions and peppers wrapped in tin foil with a little olive oil. A side dish of rice, salad, and some garlic bread toasted on the grill would frequently round out a great supper. I also got into the habit of roasting vegetables as well: zucchini, yellow squash, broccoli, corn on the cob, carrots, parsnips, you name it.

Maybe it's grilled food, or maybe it's because I was active all day, but those dinners were some of the best I ever had. I would sit out on the porch, open a beer, and have dinner while listening to the calls of the wood thrush or the hoot of an owl. The only thing I could imagine that might be better to eat, according to every mountain man I'd studied, was buffalo. Those mountain men would do anything for fresh young buffalo, savoring the liver and tongue. (Surprisingly, they seemed relatively healthy considering their diet consisted almost entirely of meat.)

On the last day of my vacation I decided to tackle cutting down the top of a big hemlock that partially blocked the view of the pond from the deck. I'd made a promise to myself never to use a chainsaw alone at the cabin. I owned one and had always tried to give it the respect it deserved. Sure, there's something macho about operating a chainsaw, but it's also dangerous, exhausting work, and my arms would usually be shaking after just twenty minutes of use. (Logging and commercial fishing are two of the most dangerous occupations in America, with fatality rates that range yearly between 1 to 1.5 workers per thousand.)

In my job as a workers' compensation underwriter, I had read enough accident reports to give me religion. There are widowmakers (dead or hung-up limbs that fall on the logger), kickbacks of the chainsaw when the tip or nose strikes an object, and kickbacks of the tree when a poor hinge is cut and the tree suddenly snaps off, sending the butt back toward the logger. Sometimes accidents are not the operator's fault, such as when a sudden gust of wind changes the direction in which the tree should fall, even when the proper wedge is cut. And sometimes it's when people do incredibly boneheaded things like lean a ladder against a sturdy branch, then climb up and cut the same branch.

The tree I wanted to cut was simply too large for my handsaw, but I figured I would just shear the top off and that would be that. I tied the handsaw around my back to free my hands and started climbing the hemlock. It was slow going because many of the lower branches were dead, and a couple of them snapped off when I stood on them. Fortunately, my hands were already around another branch and I was able to continue upward.

Sawing the top of the tree seemed to take forever; I couldn't get any leverage with one hand wrapped around the hemlock. (Remembering the victim who sawed off the branch his ladder was on, I made sure to grip the tree below where I was making the cut.) Finally the top of the tree started to lean, and with a low groan toppled over and down the cliff. Mission accomplished.

I stayed up there for a minute breathing in the evergreen-scented air, taking in the view, and feeling elated as if I were an eagle surveying my domain. I recalled how John Muir once climbed to the top of a giant tree during a wind-driven rainstorm and sang old Scottish songs, releasing his joy to the universe. For a moment I pondered doing the same, but I didn't know any Scottish songs and wisely passed.

I soon learned that climbing down a tree can be more difficult than going up, especially if you have snapped off many of the tree limbs on the upward climb. I was able to descend only ten feet from my perch when I hit a section of the tree that was trunk only, with no branches to grip. The only way to continue was to hug the tree with both arms and legs and slowly lower myself to the next branch about ten feet below. Besides the thought of being scraped to a bloody pulp, I didn't think I could securely grip the tree long enough to inch my way down. And down was forty feet.

This was dangerous. If I fell, no one was within a quarter mile to hear my screams, assuming I could scream after a fall like that. So I sat up in the tree, trying to remain calm and think things through. Staying in the tree was not an option, since it would be three or four days before I was missed by anyone down in Boston and Millie never kept track of my whereabouts. Sliding down the tree might get me to the bottom, but in what kind of shape? I'd be severely scraped and probably cut from branch nubs, and with my luck would make it halfway and then my arms would give out.

There was one other alternative, and I mulled it over for several minutes trying to calculate the odds for success. Another large hemlock grew next to the one I was in, and it had plenty of branches for an easy descent. But getting to the tree while forty feet above the ground was a risky proposition. I'd have to edge toward it with my feet on one branch and hands on one above, then make a one-foot jump to the adjacent tree, where a large branch extended toward me. Now one foot doesn't sound like much, but if the leap failed I would drop like a stone to probable death. (How did those circus trapeze guys and gals do it? Oh yeah, they had a net.)

Again I reviewed my options: Shimmying down the tree meant I'd be cut to ribbons if I didn't lose my grip and fall; whereas, making the leap from my tree to the next meant an injury-free descent, so long as I successfully made the transfer. If not, I'd probably die. What would you do? (Answering that you would have hired a professional tree guy to cut the tree down in the first place is not an option to this question.)

I started edging out on my branch toward the neighboring hemlock, testing my theory of the one-foot leap. With each inch, however, my branch drooped—something I hadn't counted on—and the one-foot leap was now more like a foot and a half.

Once, I looked down and got dizzy and immediately put all my focus on the adjacent tree, thinking that its sweeping branches were welcoming me. (I did not stop to consider that I had just cut off the top of its lifelong neighbor.) I went as far as I could, said a quick prayer, and, taking my hands off the branch above, pushed off toward my goal. My hands caught the branch perfectly, but as my legs followed, their extra weight caused one hand to slip.

Fortunately one of my feet was near a sturdy branch, and I was able to transfer some of my weight. I climbed down without incident, knowing I was a lucky idiot. The incident taught me a lesson about opting on the side of caution when alone in the woods, but when you're in your twenties, it seems you act first and think second.

I was drenched in sweat from both exertion and fear, thinking about the potential consequences for my tree-cutting actions. For a moment, I considered immediately loading my gear in my car and heading home, spooked by the thought of almost dying alone. Instead I gathered enough composure to hike down to the pond first, where, although it was fall, I stripped and dove in, letting the chilly waters of the pond wash away my self-doubt and apprehension. Once I toweled off, I decided to wander the shoreline and circle my property. The calming effects of the water and the walk got me back in a positive frame of mind, and it was fun to see parts of the woods I had not walked through in a couple of years. At different places I recalled where I'd seen wildlife, such as the spotted fawn lying motionless by a fallen birch or the time a red fox trotted by me in the hemlock grove as if I wasn't even there.

I also thought of the scheme I hatched with Boomer about selling off three of my acres. Which three would I sell? Where would the fawn and fox live if someone cleared the woods and put up a big vacation home? Maybe the scare from the tree had me in a thankful, sentimental state of mind, but I knew I couldn't sell any of the acres without regret and decided the house outside Boston could wait.

Before Boomer left that week, he did make a couple of astute observations in the guest book:

> *Between the bull on the Lamoille and the farting waitress, I should have known our road trip would be a strange one.*

> *In the tent, Toug kept me awake sniveling and complaining, "Boomer I can't sleep. I'm freezing. Where's the schnapps? Maybe I should sleep in the car. Boomer, are you listening? I can't sleep, aren't you freezing?" On he went through the night, while I slumbered soundly, snoring lightly, dreaming of lunker browns, rainbows, and smallmouths I will skillfully and cunningly angle for the next day.*

# CHAPTER 14

# OLD FRIENDS ARE
# THE BEST FRIENDS

*The ornaments of our house are the friends that frequent it.*
—RALPH WALDO EMERSON

Trips to the cabin began to follow a pattern each year, with Boomer and Cogs usually accompanying me on the first trip after the long winter, and then I mostly came alone to write. There was one cabin opening in late April during my sixth year of ownership that was particularly memorable, the trouble starting even before we stepped foot in the cabin. On that trip Boomer and I drove up early in my ancient VW Rabbit, and Cogs was coming up alone the next day.

When Boomer and I reached the cabin's "driveway," I pulled over to park by the edge of the pond.

"What are you doing?" asked Boomer.

"I'm parking here like we always do this time of year. You know my driveway is a quagmire of mud."

"Well, it's about time we at least drive up as far as we can. We've got all these groceries and gear to carry."

"All right, but I guarantee you the spot at the base of the hill will be all mud."

Boomer rolled the window down and then squeezed most of

143

his body outside. His head was above the roof of the car. "I can see everything from up here!" he shouted. "All right, let's take her up!"

I started up the driveway and had no trouble at all, feeling glad I'd listened to Boomer. Where the road dipped I expected to see standing water in the mud, but didn't see anything out of the ordinary. Still, I started to slow down, figuring it best to get out and scout by foot.

"Don't slow down!" hollered Boomer from above. "We'll make it right over that spot if you pick up speed! All clear!"

One might think that having spent twenty-two out of the twenty-eight years of my life with someone who thinks "appalling" means "appealing," the words "all clear" might not really mean "all is clear." But for some inexplicable reason—perhaps because I was anxious to see the cabin after a winter's absence—I listened to my red-haired friend and gunned the engine.

It's amazing how mud can bring a car going ten miles per hour to a dead stop in a split second. It was equally amazing that somehow Boomer managed to cling to the car's frame and was not pitched headfirst out of the window into the mud. Together, these two events ruined my afternoon. Getting stuck in the mud would have been well worth the headache if I could have seen Boomer go flying through the air like the canoe he forgot to strap onto my car a few years back.

I tried putting the car in low gear and giving it full gas, but the tires only spun, kicking mud out the rear. Boomer was shaking his head.

"I can't believe it. I just can't friggin' believe it. It looked fine and now there's a foot of mud."

He tried to open the door, but it wouldn't budge. "Make that two feet."

My door opened, but the mud was right up to the floorboards. I started to take a step out but then decided I better remove my shoes and socks. The freezing mud oozed between my toes and went halfway up my shin. I finally eased my way out of it and started walking up the driveway.

"Where you going?" shouted Boomer.

"To the cabin. There's a shovel up there."

Two trees lay across the driveway, indicating it had been a rough winter. Ferns and a few shoots of green brightened an otherwise drab brown woods that had not yet sprung to life after the harsh mountain winter.

Every time I walk my driveway, I hear the admonishment of a distant neighbor who, looking at my leaf-covered road, once said, "The other owners raked the entire road each fall and spring," implying that I should do the same. *Rake the road,* I thought, *it's almost a quarter mile long!*

The first year, I actually did just that and, yes, the road looked very spiffy—but I did not. It took me half a day, and I decided I had not bought this cabin to come here and rake, an activity I had plenty of experience with, having cleaned my parents' yard for many years. So from that time forward, leaves covered the road, and the neighbor who gave that not so gentle suggestion said it only one more time before she knew it was a lost cause.

I did, however, do an annual clearing of the road each spring, removing fallen trees and branches and cutting back the maple and beech saplings and branches that surged toward the strip of driveway. How hard the plants of the woods fight to fill a place where the sun shines, even if only for an hour each day. When a space does open up, whether by human hand or nature, it's a free-for-all, with trees and plants of infinite varieties rising toward the light. The tree that only grew a couple of inches each year in the shade now shoots up two or three feet in a single season.

If I did not cut back the trees, I estimate that in just four or five years a passerby would not be able to see any signs of the road. I kept the trees at bay using a scythe for the small ones and pruning shears for the bigger ones. I enjoyed the work immensely, especially the methodical swinging of the scythe as I worked the road from top to bottom. Activities like that are one of life's pleasures, and there were few things finer than waking up on a spring morning at the cabin, drinking my cup of coffee, and surveying the road with scythe in hand, planning the day's work. I would begin cutting, removing layers of clothing as I made my way down the hill, feeling alive in a glow of sweat from the simple physical labor. As I worked, the sweet scent of ferns, some of which were cut by the scythe, filled the still morning air with their earthy fragrance. Back and forth I'd swing the blade, until the weariness in my arms caused my cuts to be less efficient and I'd drop the scythe. I'd wipe my brow and walk up the road to my water bottle and take a long pull, thinking I had never tasted anything quite so good.

As I approached the cabin, my thoughts shifted from the anticipation of the annual road clearing to the more immediate concern: getting the car out of the mud.

The first trip up the cabin road each spring is always filled with a little trepidation that the cabin may not be standing. I worry about fire, or that a strong wind has blown the entire cabin over the cliff into the pond, or that several feet of snow have caved in the walls, even though none of these catastrophes were likely. Still, as I rounded the last bend, I was relieved to once again see the cabin perched high on its hilltop.

I crossed the front of the cabin to get a look at the pond, and my eyes went up to the second floor, where I noticed the broken window above the porch. *Could be vandals,* I thought, but more likely the culprit was a blowing branch.

When I entered the cabin it had a strange odor—far more offensive than the usual musty smell from being closed up all winter. Then I heard a heavy thud followed by some scratching. Something—or someone—was upstairs. I slowly walked to the electrical box on the back wall. Turning the circuit breakers on, I expected the lights to follow, but the electricity was dead—a tree had probably knocked down the outside wires. (Even on the sunniest of days the cabin is dark inside, because the hemlocks and white birches form a canopy above.) I grabbed a flashlight, pulled down the folding stairs, and took my first step. Something moved again up above, something a lot bigger than a mouse. I was about to turn and run, but I stood my ground, thinking this is my cabin. I took a couple more steps. The smell was overpowering, and again I hesitated before my head cleared the second floor.

I took another step and, using my flashlight, slowly scanned the second floor, half expecting a fisher or an owl to leap onto my head. Something was living there, that much was true. Insulation had been ripped from the walls, and an awful smell emanated from a pile of scat. I held my nose and took the final steps upward. Nothing stirred. Amazingly, the scat was all in a neat pile in a corner of the room on top of a large folded tarp I kept there. To remove the mess all I had to do was pick up the tarp, roll it up, and carry it down.

I disposed of the droppings fifty yards into the woods, then descended the driveway to tell Boomer we had a guest for the weekend.

Boomer was still sitting in the car, reading the paper.

"Where's the shovel?" he asked.

"Oh shoot, I forgot all about it. Got preoccupied by a visitor to the cabin."

"What?"

"The upstairs window is broken and something moved in." I hesitated a moment. "All indications are that it's just a little squirrel, so maybe together we can shoo it out of there." My strategy to get help did not work.

"If you think I'm going up to that second floor, you're crazy. I wouldn't even go up there when it was pest-free."

I wished I had gone ahead with an improvement Cogs had suggested the first time he saw the cabin: open up the second floor and make it into a loft.

"Well," I said, "we've got two problems as I see it. We're stuck in the mud with nightfall closing in, and we have a wild animal living in the cabin."

"Which should lead us," said Boomer, "to only one conclusion."

"What's that?"

"Get a hotel room."

"And just leave the cabin to the creature? No way."

Silence. "How about this," I said, "we walk down the pond road and find a house with a phone. We'll call a tow truck, and I'll also call Cogs and have him bring up his Have-a-Heart trap when he comes up tomorrow."

"But where will we sleep tonight?"

"We've got that old tent in the cabin. We'll pitch it in front of the cabin until we catch whatever it is."

"Or until it kills us."

The tow-truck operator sucked on his cigarette while surveying our car in the mud.

"Is the mud seeping into the car?" he asked.

"Not yet," I answered.

"Who was driving?"

I didn't think this question was pertinent to getting our car unstuck, so I ignored him.

Boomer was only too helpful. "He was," he said, pointing at me.

"And you didn't see this mud pit?" asked the tow man.

Before I could respond and say Boomer told me it was OK, the man continued. "This little swale in the road is a regular mud trap. All the water from the upper road rolls down here and collects, not giving the ground a chance to dry."

I did not need a lecture on the hydraulics of water and mud, so I said, "Let's just pull it out."

While the tow-truck operator was hooking up, another man, whom I had never seen before, sauntered along the pond road and turned into my road.

"Wow, you're really in there but good."

The tow-truck operator had everything hooked up and within a minute popped the car from the ooze. As I paid him, he said, "Don't try to go through there again."

I said, "Thanks," while giving Boomer a menacing look.

Boomer and I turned our attention back to the car. We began to unload gear from the trunk, arranging it on the ground for the safari up the hill. Boomer was in high spirits, saying, "I feel great—put some of that gear on my head."

Caught up in the mood of goodwill, I responded, "Why, that's mighty neighborly of you. No need for my good buddy to do all the work." Then I slapped him on the back in a gesture of brotherly love.

Somehow Boomer took the slap on the back to mean that we

were finished unloading the trunk, so he slammed the trunk door down . . . right on my thumb.

Only the tip of my thumb was caught, and I yanked it out, howling. "You fool, my thumb! Look at my thumb! Look at it! It's flat!"

"Oh God, I'm sorry," said Boomer, "I didn't see it."

I danced around, holding my thumb, every now and then looking at it and screaming, "It's totally flat!"

Boomer came over for a closer look. "It's not totally flat. You're actually lucky, it's just the tip and not the knuckle."

*Lucky?* I thought. *Oh, yes I'm blessed with good fortune. I'm out fifty dollars for a tow truck, a creature has taken over my cabin, and my thumb is as flat as a pancake.*

The entry I made in the guest book that night read:

> *Boomer got the car stuck in the mud and then closed the trunk on my thumb. But the real problem is that something is living upstairs. When I first went up there I spotted the latrine in the corner, which was enough to make the hairs on my neck stand out, not to mention make me nauseous. Yes, something as big as a dog is living on the second floor.*

We slept in the tent that night. In the morning we headed straight to our favorite fishing spot on the Lamoille River, then out to breakfast. An old-timer in the restaurant saw us walk in with our waders on and immediately said, "Hey Four-eyes [meaning me] and Slim [meaning Boomer, who's a bit chunky], come on over here a second."

"You catch anything?"

"Nothing yet," I said, "I think it's a little cold."

"Cold?" he bellowed, "For who? You or the trout? It's not too cold; you two just don't know what you're doing, I'll wager. What are you using?"

Boomer answered "flies" and I replied "spinners."

"Well, no wonder all you're catching is colds! No trout in its right mind is going to be on the surface sipping flies or going hog-wild chasing some fool spinner."

Half the restaurant was listening in on this verbal tongue-lashing, and I suspect it wasn't the first time this gent had set a couple of young men straight. He was holding court, only now he needed to solidify his standing with us and give out his credentials. He lowered his head and motioned us closer with his hand.

In a low voice he said, "Listen, I've been known to be in the possession of over a hundred trout. I just stack 'em up in my waders. You look like good guys, so I'm going to give you a little tip. Forget the spinners and flies. What you boys got to do is go deep. Find the deepest pool and lay down a gob of night crawlers. Be sure they're night crawlers and not some skinny worms."

Boomer and I thanked him, anxious to sit down and get some hot coffee in us.

We found a booth in the back and I leaned over to Boomer. "Now I know why we haven't caught anything."

"Why, 'cause we're not using gobs of night crawlers?"

"No, 'cause that old codger has taken all the fish out of the river."

After Cogs arrived I went into the dark attic, carrying a flashlight, the Have-a-Heart trap, and a jar of peanut butter. I still had no idea what was up there, but I figured everything likes peanut butter and used it to bait the trap. Then I joined Cogs and Boomer by the fire.

Real mountain men had annual rendezvous, where after being solo in the mountains for a year living off the land and trapping, they were happy to meet up with other trappers and party for a few days. I thought maybe we could do something similar since it was a Friday night.

But as I approached the fire, Cogs and Boomer stood up.

"Time to turn in," said Boomer.

"What?" I said, shocked that Boomer, who was always game for a party, wanted to hit the sack.

"I'm exhausted," he said. "We've been up since five this morning fishing, and I think I'm getting a cold."

Cogs piped in, "Me, too. My back's sore from all that driving."

"But what about sitting by the fire?" I whined. "It's tradition."

"We'll take a rain check," said Cogs, "plus, it's cold out here."

*Some mountain men,* I thought to myself as they went into the tent. *What wimps; too cold, too tired.* I doubt Kit Carson ever passed up a rendezvous because he had the sniffles.

So I sat by the fire alone. My thumb was throbbing and I felt a chill from the night air. Now that Boomer had said he felt like he was getting a cold, my throat felt a little scratchy. *It's really not worth staying up alone,* I thought. A wise mountaineer knows when to get proper rest. I took two Tylenol and headed into the tent.

At about two in the morning, a loud bang woke all of us up, followed by terrible clanging sounds coming from inside the cabin.

"Toug," said Cogs, with a little quiver in his voice, "I think you caught something."

Judging from the sounds of it, I had caught something big.

Boomer was sitting up. "Geez, will you listen to that thing? It's time for the great hunter to see what it is." Boomer was looking at me.

"Who's coming with me?"

Boomer lay back down and put his pillow over his head. Cogs started to do the same.

"Don't you want to know what it is?" I asked Cogs.

"Not really. It can wait till morning."

"Listen to it."

The banging had not subsided. I assumed the creature was in the cage going nuts. What if only part of it were in the cage, or what if there were more than one?

"Cogs," I said, "there's no way you're going to get any sleep with that thing going nuts. Let's go get it out of there."

Cogs sat back up. "OK, I'll go in with you, but I'm taking a club."

"Here, take this flashlight too," I said helpfully. "Remember, the electricity is dead."

Inside the cabin, it sounded like there was a barroom brawl upstairs.

"I'll poke my head up," said Cogs, "but that's as far as I go."

I was relieved he was going first. That way if the thing was still loose, it would latch itself onto his face first and I could flee.

Cogs took a couple of steps up the stairs and the noise quickly stopped, and so did Cogs.

"You can do it, Cogs," I said, thinking, *Now here's a real mountain man, not like that frightened rabbit hiding in the tent with his pillow over his head.*

Cogs went up another step, which was enough for his head to clear the second floor. A terrible growl sounded overhead and I backed away from the ladder.

"Oh my God", said Cogs slowly. *"You've* caught a big old raccoon."

*Damn,* I thought, I'd been hoping for a squirrel. This was not good. Another thing I didn't like was the way Cogs said, *"You've* caught a big old raccoon." We all caught it. Don't forget, Cogs is the one who brought the trap up.

"So now what?" I asked.

"Go up and take a look," said Cogs, stepping off the stairs. "That thing is huge, and it ain't happy."

I really didn't want to go up. No, I thought, we should all just let bygones be bygones, and the raccoon could go its way and I mine. But the raccoon was in the trap in my cabin.

I climbed the stairs, shining the flashlight at the raccoon. Its beady eyes glared at me and it showed its teeth. Then it made a quick move, crashing into the side of the trap. For an instant I thought it would get free and I jumped backward.

"What happened?" shouted Cogs from below.

"This thing is wild." *No kidding,* I thought to myself after I said it. "Cogs, I'm afraid it's going to tip this trap over and get out."

"Well, then carry it down."

"Are you crazy? That raccoon must weigh a hundred pounds and the trap is four feet across. How am I going to get it down these narrow stairs."

"Here, take this."

I reached down the stairway and he handed me a blanket. Gingerly, I moved toward the trap and tried to drape it over the top.

The raccoon went into a snarling frenzy, grabbing the blanket through the cage openings with its forefeet and ripping it to shreds with its teeth. I stared wide-eyed, ready to flee down the stairs. The raccoon reminded me of a small grizzly bear, and I thought of Meriwether Lewis being charged by a grizzly on the Platte River. That bear image actually gave me a little bit of courage, and I stood my ground. I had dealt with my fear of bears, and I could handle this.

"Cogs," I commanded, "get me some of those large pieces of slate from the fire pit. I want to put them on top of the trap so it can't tip over."

Cogs, recognizing my newfound authority, did as he was told, and we secured the raccoon until morning. We went back to the tent to get some shut-eye.

But the raccoon had other plans. It banged against the cage, making such a racket it was impossible to sleep. I also felt a sense of pity for the caged raccoon, knowing this wasn't the way it had planned to spend the night. After tossing and turning for an hour, I had finally had enough and started walking down the dirt driveway, dragging my sleeping bag behind me like a demented adult version of Linus from the *Peanuts* comic strip. I wasn't heading anywhere in particular, simply walking until I could no longer hear the raccoon. Then I laid my sleeping bag down in the woods, crawled inside, and fell asleep under the stars.

When I awoke four beady eyes were staring down at me. Through the fog and gray light of dawn, I could just make out two heads, and they were horrifying. They were also close enough that I could hear their breathing and smell their foul breath. I hoped it was all a nightmare—I did not want to confront these creatures who had discovered my resting place in the woods.

The one with the red hair spoke. "You're pathetic. Look at you lying in the middle of the woods."

The tall, thin one joined in. "Get up, you wretched thing. Your raccoon awaits."

I rolled over and propped my head on tree root. Slowly the events of last night came back to me. *Oh no*, I thought, *that raccoon is still up there.*

As if reading my mind, Cogs said, "It's not thrashing around as much, but every now and then it seems to get a burst of energy. The safest thing to do would be to just shoot it in the trap."

"Well, if you can borrow a gun from one of my neighbors, be my guest."

"I'm hungry," said Boomer, "Let's go out for breakfast first."

"Good idea," said Cogs, "we can figure out a strategy over banana walnut pancakes."

After dozens of pancakes and gallons of coffee, we came to a consensus. We would hire an exterminator to get the raccoon out of the cabin and out of the trap.

I used the phone outside the restaurant and called a local "pest control professional," somewhat embarrassed to admit that we had caught the raccoon but didn't want to pick up the cage.

The exterminator tried to put me at ease. "I don't blame you. Those things can be nasty."

"This one in particular," I added.

"And you've got to be careful around raccoons; they can be prone to rabies and their scat can have parasites that can be deadly to humans. I try to never touch raccoons, even with gloves on."

I thought of the pile of droppings I had removed from the cabin.

The exterminator said he would meet us at the restaurant and follow us up to the cabin. He agreed to "dispose" of the raccoon, telling me it was illegal to move and release one that had been trapped. He would leave the empty trap at his house and we could pick it up later.

When we all arrived at the cabin, I decided to pay him in advance so I wouldn't have to witness any of this sad affair. Even though it had trashed my cabin, I still felt bad for the raccoon. Why couldn't it have found another home? Six acres of woods, complete with hollow trees, fallen logs, and rocky crevices, and this raccoon had to pick my cabin. The whole thing made me depressed. I did not come here to do battle. Wildlife was one reason I picked this spot. I came here to be with the wildlife, observe it, marvel at it . . . but not sleep with it.

Boomer sensed my gloom and made a wise observation. "Look on the bright side. Last night was your first night sleeping all alone in the woods with no tent, no knife, and no friends. You're lucky some bear didn't drag you off."

Lucky? Actually, I really was.

Cogs's entry in the guest book summed up the experience:

*Finding Toug asleep in the woods made the affair with the raccoon almost worth it. Also, why was I able to make it through the mud at the bottom of the hill when Toug and Boomer sank? Poor navigation by Toug, I think.*

# CHAPTER 15

# GO SLOW, GO DEEP

*I'm faced with the challenge of change month in and month out, but the cabin trips are a welcome constant in my life.*
—COGS

After the exterminator left, things slowly returned to normal that day. We fished (caught nothing), took a freezing jump in the pond, and hiked a nearby mountain range. It was too early for blackflies, yet the temperature climbed into the sixties, making it a perfect spring day. We even got back to tradition—a campfire and celebrating with a well-deserved beer.

While Cogs started fixing dinner on the gas grill, Boomer and I carried the big oak chairs outside and arranged them around the fire. Boomer kicked off the conversation.

"My dad asked me what we do up here. When I said we 'roughed it' and fished, he burst out laughing and said, 'You three cream puffs couldn't survive a day without all your little comforts.'"

"He's right," I said.

"If we had to, we could survive up here for a week or two."

"Maybe," I answered. "But when I said 'he's right,' I meant the part about us being cream puffs."

"Does your dad ever get up here?" Boomer asked.

"Naw, but he always says that just knowing this place is here is enough for him. Even if he wanted to, he couldn't get up, because he takes care of my sister."

"How long's it been since her accident?"

"It happened right before I bought the cabin, about six years ago."

We looked into the flames, and I thought how unfair life could be, how my sister had never been to the cabin due to severe injuries she had suffered in a car accident.

"You know," I said, "while I was on the river, I watched a king-fisher glide over the water. It was beautiful. And that jump we took in the pond was freezing, but boy did I feel great when I got out. I just like to float in the pond and look up at the clouds. I love the way the blue sky and white clouds slowly pass over the tops of the spruces. Seems like nobody bothers to notice that stuff anymore; everybody's too busy trying to make money."

"Nothing wrong with a little money, but I know what you mean."

"Sometimes I wish I could take total strangers up here—people who don't give a damn about the outdoors—and let them experience these little things. Then I think they'd go back with a sense of appreciation."

"What are you going to do with the place? Do you think you'll always keep it?"

I thought about that one for a while. When I had bought the place I had felt the joy of possession, of being the king of my dominion. Now I had something more like a personal attachment to the land, a feeling so strong I was beginning to think about putting conservation restrictions on the property so that when I'm long gone, this hill, this pond, and these trees will be the same as they are now.

I got around to answering Boomer's question. "Yeah, I think I'll always keep it, pass it down to my kids."

"Kids?" he said incredulously. "We can't even get girlfriends."

"You know what I mean. Someday both of us might be coming up here with our kids." The thought of kids made me think how crowded the world was getting. Even here I noticed a couple of new homes going up each year near my favorite fishing spots. "And if I do have children," I added, "I'm only having two. We're like rabbits breeding ourselves out of house and home."

"You're getting way too deep on me. And you're way off in the future. I'm just trying to enjoy the here and now before I have to go back to work."

Boomer was right, so I changed the subject. "Do you remember our first trip up here?"

"How could I forget? I believe my record for the largest trout still stands."

"You know, it was right after that trip that I started writing. My first piece was about spring fishing in Vermont. Now that I think about it, the man at the restaurant said the same thing my article did; fish deep and slow."

"We're starting to forget everything we learned about fishing. Is that a sign of senility?"

"Could be. I also think it just means we don't care as much about catching fish as we used to. I think we like to walk the river, which is why we don't stay in one spot and fish deep."

Boomer was still thinking about his first trip to the cabin, and he asked, "Wasn't that first trip when you bought the pink bike? Whatever happened to it?"

"It's still in the cabin. I put it up on the second floor, but every now and then I take it out for a spin. Got to keep my image up with the neighbors."

Boomer laughed and, using his foot, moved another log into the fire. "My favorite thing up here is this part, right now. Sitting by a campfire. I'm tired, but it's a good kind of tired."

"Yup," I said.

"Speaking of sleep," said Boomer, "you should try sleeping in the woods again. You looked very comfortable there. You could be a real mountain man and come up and just wander the woods with a knapsack."

"Naw, I'm over that mountain-man macho stuff. I'm happy sleeping on the porch."

Besides, I thought to myself, the mountain-man idea wasn't the right one. Rather than "conquering the land," I had learned to let the woods teach me, feeling a renewal of my spirit from the stillness and the beauty that was waiting in the outdoors. The cabin allowed me to step outside my everyday life, escape the trappings of the world we live in, and instead fill me with new experiences. Like fishing, it taught me to go slow and to go deep.

# EPILOGUE

I'm sitting on the cabin deck looking off at the mountains, watching the sun go down. The distant mountain range is shadowed, but the ridge directly across the pond is still bathed in light and a lone birch tree reflects the last rays of the sun, shining like a beacon.

The first owl of the night calls, "Who cooks for you, who cooks for you?" A wood thrush sings its melancholy song, and a bullfrog down in the pond announces its presence. A red squirrel chatters from a nearby hemlock, and something is scraping leaves on the knoll in front of the cabin. I love all these sounds.

Over the years I have learned. I know the owl calling is a barred owl, and I know from the scat I've been finding that a bear might visit the raspberry patch behind the cabin tonight, unseen but welcome. Maybe even a porcupine will shuffle by the outhouse.

I think of how things have changed since my twenties. In my book *The Waters Between Us*, something of a prequel to this book, I described how I bought the cabin on Christmas Eve 1978. At that time, I only thought a year or two ahead and couldn't fathom that I'd be coming to the cabin for over forty years, and that I'd watch my two kids, Kristin and Brian, grow to love the place as I do.

Many visitors have come—some never to return because a remote cabin was not their cup of tea, while others have felt right at home and make a trip to the cabin a kind of pilgrimage.

Some of my best trips have been alone. I'm not the fishing fanatic I was, more content to wander the woods, swim the pond, and take advantage of the solitude to work on one of my book projects. The cabin has been my anchor, helping me through tough times and making the good times even better. Cogs recently said that despite all the changes in his life, the trips to the cabin are the one constant, something he's grown to rely on. I feel the same.

I'm comfortable in the woods now, those early fears having long since melted away. I often feel like the luckiest man alive.

# About the Author

**Michael J. Tougias** (pronounced TOH-gis) is a lecturer and *New York Times* best-selling author and coauthor of thirty-one books for adults and eight for young adults and children.

*Fatal Forecast: An Incredible True Tale of Disaster and Survival at Sea* was praised by the *Los Angeles Times* as "a breathtaking book—Tougias spins a marvelous and terrifying story." *The Finest Hours*, which Tougias coauthored, tells the true story of the Coast Guard's most daring rescue. A finalist for the Massachusetts Book Award, the book was made into a movie by Disney. *Ten Hours Until Dawn: The True Story of Heroism and Tragedy Aboard the Can Do in the Blizzard of 78*, was selected by the American Library Association as one of the "Top Books of the Year" and described as a "white-knuckle read, the best book of its kind." His latest books are *A Storm Too Soon, Above & Beyond*, and a prequel to *There's a Porcupine in My Outhouse* titled *The Waters Between Us: A Boy, A Father, Outdoor Misadventures, and the Healing Power of Nature.*

Several of Tougias's books were adapted for middle readers (ages 8–13) and for chapter books with MacMillan Publishers. His series is "The True Rescue Series" and it includes *Into the Blizzard, Attacked At Sea, A Storm Too Soon*, and *The Finest Hours*.

Michael Tougias has been featured on ABC's *20/20*, the Weather Channel, and NPR, among other appearances. He offers slide lectures for each of his books and speaks at libraries, lecture series, schools, and colleges across the country. He also speaks to business groups and associations on leadership and decision-making, including such programs as Leadership Lessons from the Finest Hours; Survival Lessons: Decision Making Under Pressure; and Fourteen Steps to Strategic Decision Making: JFK and the Cuban Missile Crisis. He lives in Florida and Massachusetts. For more information, videos of some of the rescues Tougias writes about, or to contact the author, visit www.michaeltougias.com.

*Tougias's most popular books include:*

**Rescue of the Bounty: A True Story of Disaster and Survival in Superstorm Sandy**, coauthor Douglas Campbell

**A Storm Too Soon: A True Story of Disaster, Survival, and an Incredible Rescue**

**Overboard! A True Blue-Water Odyssey of Disaster and Survival**

**Fatal Forecast: An Incredible True Story of Disaster and Survival at Sea**

**Ten Hours Until Dawn: The True Story of Heroism and Tragedy Aboard the Can Do**

**The Finest Hours: The True Story of the US Coast Guard's Most Daring Sea Rescue**, coauthor Casey Sherman

**The Waters Between Us: A Boy, A Father, Outdoor Misadventures, and the Healing Power of Nature**

**Until I Have No Country: A Novel of King Philip's Indian War**

**King Philip's War: The History and Legacy of America's Forgotten Conflict**, coauthor Eric Schultz

**Above & Beyond: John F. Kennedy and America's Most Dangerous Spy Mission**, coauthor Casey Sherman

**There's a Porcupine in My Outhouse: Misadventures of a Mountain Man Wannabe**

**So Close to Home: A True Story of an American Family's Fight for Survival During WWII**, coauthor Alison O'Leary

**River Days: Exploring the Connecticut River from Source to Sea**

*AMC's Best Day Hikes Near Boston*

*Exploring the Hidden Charles*

*Country Roads of Massachusetts*

*Quiet Places of Massachusetts*

*New England Wild Places*

*The Cringe Chronicles*, coauthor Kristin Tougias

*Quabbin: A History and Explorers Guide*

*The Blizzard of '78*

Middle reader adaptations: *The Finest Hours*, *A Storm Too Soon*, *Attacked At Sea*, *Into the Blizzard*, and *Claws*